W9-CHL-221

HOLT
SCIENCE &
TECHNOLOGY

Environmental Science

HOLT, RINEHART AND WINSTON

A Harcourt Education Company

Orlando • **Austin** • New York • San Diego • Toronto • London

Acknowledgments

Contributing Authors

Katy Z. Allen
Science Writer
Wayland, Massachusetts

Linda Ruth Berg, Ph.D.
Adjunct Professor of Natural Sciences
St. Petersburg College
St. Petersburg, Florida

Robert H. Fronk, Ph.D.
Chair of Science and Mathematics Education
Florida Institute of Technology
West Melbourne, Florida

Inclusion and Special Needs Consultant

Ellen McPeek Glisan
Special Needs Consultant
San Antonio, Texas

Safety Reviewer

Jack Gerlovich, Ph.D.
Associate Professor
School of Education
Drake University
Des Moines, Iowa

Academic Reviewers

Glenn Adelson, Ph.D.
Instructor
Biology Undergraduate Program
Harvard University
Cambridge, Massachusetts

John Brockhaus, Ph.D.
Director of Geospatial Science Information Program
Department of Geography and Environmental Engineering
United States Military Academy
West Point, New York
University of Minnesota
Duluth, Minnesota

Joel S. Leventhal, Ph.D.
Emeritus Scientist, Geochemistry
U.S. Geological Survey
Lakewood, Colorado

Eva Oberdoerster, Ph.D.
Lecturer
Department of Biology
Southern Methodist University
Dallas, Texas

Teacher Reviewers

Diedre S. Adams
Physical Science Instructor
West Vigo Middle School
West Terre Haute, Indiana

Barbara Gavin Akre
Teacher of Biology, Anatomy-Physiology, and Life Science
Duluth Independent School District
Duluth, Minnesota

Sarah Carver
Science Teacher
Jackson Creek Middle School
Bloomington, Indiana

Hilary Cochran
Science Teacher
Indian Crest Junior High School
Souderton, Pennsylvania

Randy Dye, M.S.
Science Department Head
Wood Middle School
Fort Leonard Wood, Missouri

Debra S. Kogelman, MAed.
Science Teacher
University of Chicago Laboratory Schools
Chicago, Illinois

Augie Maldonado
Science Teacher
Grisham Middle School
Round Rock, Texas

Marci L. Stadiem
Science Department Head
Cascade Middle School
Seattle, Washington

Florence Vaughan
Science Teacher
University of Chicago Laboratory Schools
Chicago, Illinois

Angie Williams
Teacher
Riversprings Middle School
Crawfordville, Florida

Lab Development

Diana Scheidle Bartos
Research Associate
School of Mines
Golden, Colorado

Carl Benson
General Science Teacher
Plains High School
Plains, Montana

Charlotte Blassingame
Technology Coordinator
White Station Middle School
Memphis, Tennessee

Marsha Carver
*Science Teacher and
    Department Chair*
McLean County
    High School
Calhoun, Kentucky

Kenneth E. Creese
Science Teacher
White Mountain Junior
    High School
Rock Springs, Wyoming

Linda A. Culp
*Science Teacher and
    Department Chair*
Thorndale High School
Thorndale, Texas

James Deaver
*Science Teacher and
    Department Chair*
West Point High School
West Point, Nebraska

Frank McKinney, Ph.D.
Professor of Geology
Appalachian State
    University
Boone, North Carolina

Alyson M. Mike
*Science Teacher and
    Department Chair*
East Valley Middle School
East Helena, Montana

C. Ford Morishita
Biology Teacher
Clackamas High School
Milwaukie, Oregon

Patricia D. Morrell, Ph.D.
Associate Professor
School of Education
University of Portland
Portland, Oregon

Hilary C. Olson, Ph.D.
Research Associate
Institute for Geophysics
The University of Texas
    at Austin
Austin, Texas

James B. Pulley
*Science Editor and Former
    Science Teacher*
North Kansas City, Missouri

Denice Lee Sandefur
Science Chairperson
Nucla High School
Nucla, Colorado

Patti Soderberg
Science Writer
The BioQUEST Curriculum
    Consortium
Biology Department
Beloit College
Beloit, Wisconsin

Phillip Vavala
*Science Teacher and
    Department Chair*
Salesianum School
Wilmington, Delaware

Albert C. Wartski, M.A.T.
Biology Teacher
Chapel Hill High School
Chapel Hill, North Carolina

Lynn Marie Wartski
*Science Writer and Former
    Science Teacher*
Hillsborough, North
    Carolina

Ivora D. Washington
*Science Teacher and
    Department Chair*
Hyattsville Middle School
Washington, D.C.

Lab Testing

Barry L. Bishop
*Science Teacher and
    Department Chair*
San Rafael Junior High
    School
Ferron, Utah

James Chin
Science Teacher
Frank A. Day Middle School
Newtonville, Massachusetts

Alonda Droege
Biology Teacher
Evergreen High School
Seattle, Washington

Tracy Jahn
Science Teacher
Berkshire Jr–Sr. High School
Canaan, New York

Kerry A. Johnson
Science Teacher
Isbell Middle School
Santa Paula, California

Jason P. Marsh
Biology Teacher
Montevideo High School
    and Montevideo Country
    School
Montevideo, Minnesota

Terry J. Rakes
Science Teacher
Elmwood Junior High
    School
Rogers, Arkansas

Debra A. Sampson
Science Teacher
Booker T. Washington
    Middle School
Elgin, Texas

David M. Sparks
Science Teacher
Redwater Junior High
    School
Redwater, Texas

Gordon Zibelman
Science Teacher
Drexel Hill Middle School
Drexel Hill, Pennsylvania

Feature Development

Hatim Belyamani
John A. Benner
David Bradford
Jennifer Childers
Mickey Coakley
Susan Feldkamp
Jane Gardner
Erik Hahn
Christopher Hess
Deena Kalai
Charlotte W. Luongo, MSc
Michael May
Persis Mehta, Ph.D.
Eileen Nehme, MPH
Catherine Podeszwa
Dennis Rathnaw
Daniel B. Sharp
April Smith West
John M. Stokes
Molly F. Wetterschneider

Answer Checking

Hatim Belyamani
Austin, Texas

E Environmental Science

Safety First! x

CHAPTER 1 Interactions of Living Things 2
  SECTION 1 Everything Is Connected 4
  SECTION 2 Living Things Need Energy 8
  SECTION 3 Types of Interactions 14
Chapter Lab Skills Practice Capturing the Wild Bean 22
Chapter Review 24
Standardized Test Preparation 26
Science in Action 28
LabBook Model Making Adaptation: It's a Way of Life 130

CHAPTER 2 Cycles in Nature 30
  SECTION 1 The Cycles of Matter 32
  SECTION 2 Ecological Succession 36
Chapter Lab Skills Practice Nitrogen Needs 40
Chapter Review 42
Standardized Test Preparation 44
Science in Action 46
LabBook Model Making A Passel o' Pioneers 132

CHAPTER ③ **The Earth's Ecosystems** 48

    SECTION 1 Land Biomes 50
    SECTION 2 Marine Ecosystems 58
    SECTION 3 Freshwater Ecosystems 64

Chapter Lab Skills Practice Too Much of a Good Thing? 68
Chapter Review 70
Standardized Test Preparation 72
Science in Action 74

LabBook **Inquiry** Life in the Desert 134
             Inquiry Discovering Mini-Ecosystems 135

CHAPTER ④ **Environmental Problems
and Solutions** 76

    SECTION 1 Environmental Problems 78
    SECTION 2 Environmental Solutions 84

Chapter Lab Inquiry Biodiversity—What a Disturbing Thought! 92
Chapter Review 94
Standardized Test Preparation 96
Science in Action 98

CHAPTER ⑤ **Energy Resources** 100

    SECTION 1 Natural Resources 102
    SECTION 2 Fossil Fuels 106
    SECTION 3 Alternative Resources 114

Chapter Lab Model Making Make a Water Wheel 122
Chapter Review 124
Standardized Test Preparation 126
Science in Action 128

LabBook **Skills Practice** Power of the Sun 136

Labs and Activities

PRE-READING ACTIVITY

FOLDNOTES

Tri-Fold 2
Pyramid 30
Three-Panel Flip Chart 48
Two-Panel Flip Chart 76

Graphic Organizer

Comparison Table 100

START-UP ACTIVITY

Who Eats Whom? 3
Making Rain 31
A Mini-Ecosystem 49
Recycling Paper 77
What Is the Sun's Favorite Color? 101

Quick Lab

Meeting the Neighbors 5
Combustion 34
Pond-Food Relationships 65
Rock Sponge 109

Labs

Skills Practice Capturing the Wild Bean 22
Skills Practice Nitrogen Needs 40
Skills Practice Too Much of a
  Good Thing? 68
Inquiry Biodiversity—What a
  Disturbing Thought! 92
Model Making Make a Water Wheel 122
Model Making Adaptation: It's a Way
  of Life 130
Model Making A Passel o' Pioneers 132
Inquiry Life in the Desert 134
Inquiry Discovering Mini-Ecosystems 135
Skills Practice Power of the Sun 136

INTERNET ACTIVITY

Go to go.hrw.com and type in the red keyword.

Chapter 1 Prairie Play HL5INTW
Chapter 2 Land Recovery HL5CYCW
Chapter 3 Earth Biome
  Brochure HL5ECOW
Chapter 4 Habitat Destruction HL5ENVW
Chapter 5 Renewable Energy
  Resources HL5ENRW

SCHOOL to HOME

A Chain Game 9
Local Ecosystems 56
Renewable? 104

READING STRATEGY

Brainstorming
Chapter 5 106
Discussion
Chapter 4 84
Mnemonics
Chapter 2 32
Paired Summarizing
Chapter 3 64
Chapter 5 114
Prediction Guide
Chapter 3 58
Reading Organizer—Concept Map
Chapter 1 14
Chapter 4 78
Chapter 5 102
Reading Organizer—Outline
Chapter 1 4
Chapter 3 50
Reading Organizer—Table
Chapter 1 8
Chapter 2 36

CONNECTION TO · · ·

Chemistry
Ozone Holes 79
Hydrocarbons 108

Environmental Science
Pretenders 17
Global Warming 35
Mountains and Climate 54

Language Arts
Compound Words 66
Resources of the Future 116

Social Studies
Rabbits in Australia 20
Wood 82

MATH PRACTICE

Energy Pyramids 13
Where's the Water? 33
Water Depletion 80
Miles per Acre 119

Science in Action

Careers
Dalton Dockery Horticulture Specialist 29
Michael Fan Wastewater Manager 47
Alfonso Alonso-Mejía Ecologist 75
Fred Begay Nuclear Physicist 129

People in Science
Phil McCrory Hairy Oil Spills 99

Science, Technology, and Society
Desalination 46
Hydrogen-Fueled Automobiles 98
Hybrid Cars 128

Scientific Debate
How Did Dogs Become Pets? 28
Developing Wetlands 74
Where Should the Wolves Roam? 98
The Three Gorges Dam 128

Scientific Discoveries
The Dead Zone 46
Ocean Vents 74

Weird Science
Follicle Mites 28

LabBook 130

Appendix 138
Reading Check Answers 138
Study Skills 140
Scientific Methods 146
Math Refresher 148

Glossary 152

Spanish Glossary 155

Index 158

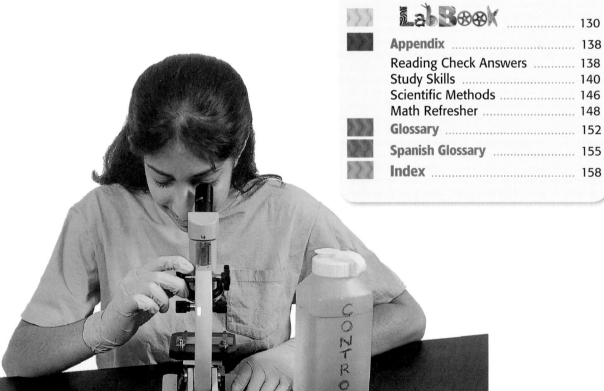

How to Use Your Textbook

Your Roadmap for Success with Holt Science and Technology

What You Will Learn

At the beginning of every section you will find the section's objectives and vocabulary terms. The objectives tell you what you'll need to know after you finish reading the section.

Vocabulary terms are listed for each section. Learn the definitions of these terms because you will most likely be tested on them. Each term is highlighted in the text and is defined at point of use and in the margin. You can also use the glossary to locate definitions quickly.

STUDY TIP Reread the objectives and the definitions to the terms when studying for a test to be sure you know the material.

Get Organized

A Reading Strategy at the beginning of every section provides tips to help you organize and remember the information covered in the section. Keep a science notebook so that you are ready to take notes when your teacher reviews the material in class. Keep your assignments in this notebook so that you can review them when studying for the chapter test.

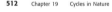

SECTION 2

Ecological Succession

Imagine you have a time machine that can take you back to the summer of 1988. If you had visited Yellowstone National Park during that year, you would have seen fires raging throughout the area.

By the end of that summer, large areas of the park were burned to the ground. When the fires were put out, a layer of gray ash blanketed the forest floor. Most of the trees were dead, although many of them were still standing.

Regrowth of a Forest

The following spring, the appearance of the "dead" forest began to change. **Figure 1** shows the changes after just one year. Some of the dead trees fell over, and small, green plants grew in large numbers. Within 10 years, scientists reported that many trees were growing and the forest community was coming back.

A gradual development of a community over time, such as the regrowth of the burned areas of Yellowstone National Park, is called **succession.** Succession takes place in all communities, not just those affected by disturbances such as forest fires.

Reading Check What happened after the Yellowstone fires? (See the Appendix for answers to Reading Checks.)

What You Will Learn
- Describe the process of succession.
- Contrast primary and secondary succession.
- Explain how mature communities develop.

Vocabulary
succession
pioneer species

READING STRATEGY

Reading Organizer As you read this section, make a table comparing primary succession and secondary succession.

succession the replacement of one type of community by another at a single place over a period of time

Figure 1 Huge areas of Yellowstone National Park were burned in 1988 (left). By the spring of 1989, regrowth was evident in the burned parts of the park (right).

512 Chapter 19 Cycles in Nature

Be Resourceful—Use the Web

SciLinks boxes in your textbook take you to resources that you can use for science projects, reports, and research papers. Go to **scilinks.org** and type in the **SciLinks code** to find information on a topic.

Visit go.hrw.com
Check out the **Current Science**® magazine articles and other materials that go with your textbook at **go.hrw.com.** Click on the textbook icon and the table of contents to see all of the resources for each chapter.

Primary Succession

Sometimes, a small community starts to grow in an area where other organisms had not previously lived. There is no soil in this area. And usually, there is just bare rock. Over a very long time, a series of organisms live and die on the rock. The rock is slowly transformed into soil. This process is called *primary succession*, as shown in **Figure 2**. The first organisms to live in an area are called **pioneer species**.

pioneer species a species that colonizes an uninhabited area and that starts a process of succession

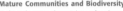
Figure 2 An Example of Primary Succession

❶ A slowly retreating glacier exposes bare rock where nothing lives, and primary succession begins.

❷ Most primary succession begins with lichens. Acids from the lichens begin breaking the rocks into small particles. These particles mix with the remains of dead lichens to start forming soil. Lichens are an example of a pioneer species.

❸ After many enough s grow. The replace th other tiny live there. remains a

Mature Communities and Biodiversity

In the early stages of succession, only a few species grow in an area. These species grow quickly and make many seeds that scatter easily. But all species are vulnerable to disease, disturbances, and competition. As a community matures, it may be dominated by well-adapted, slow-growing *climax species*.

Furthermore, as succession proceeds, more species may become established. The variety of species that are present in an area is referred to as *biodiversity*. Biodiversity is important to communities of organisms. For example, a forest that has a high degree of biodiversity is less likely to be destroyed by an invasion of insects. Most plant-damaging insects prefer to attack only one species of plants. The presence of a variety of plants will lessen the impact and spread of invading insects.

Keep in mind that a mature community may not always be a forest. A mature community simply has organisms that are well adapted to live together in the same area over time. For example, the plants of the Sonoran Desert, shown in **Figure 4**, are well-adapted to the desert's conditions.

Figure 4 This area of the Sonoran Desert in Arizona is a mature community.

SECTION Review

Summary

● Ecological succession is the gradual development of communities over time. Often a series of stages is observed during succession.

● Primary succession occurs in an area that was not previously inhabited by living things; no soil is present.

● Secondary succession takes place in an area where an earlier community was disturbed by fire, landslides, floods, or plowing for crops and where soil is present.

Using Key Terms

1. In your own words, write a definition for the term *succession*.

Understanding Key Ideas

2. An area where a glacier has just melted away will begin the process of
   a. primary succession.
   b. secondary succession.
   c. stability.
   d. regrowth.

3. Describe succession that takes place in an abandoned field.

4. Describe a mature community. How does a mature community develop?

Math Skills

5. The fires in 1988 burned 739,000 of the 2.2 million acres that make up Yellowstone National Park. What percentage of the park was burned?

Critical Thinking

6. **Applying Concepts** Give an example of a community that has a high degree of biodiversity, and an example of one that has a low degree of biodiversity.

7. **Analyzing Ideas** Explain why soil formation is always the first stage of primary succession. Does soil formation ever stop? Explain your answer.

SCILINKS.

NSTA Developed and maintained by the National Science Teachers Association

For a variety of links related to this chapter, go to **www.scilinks.org**

Topic: Succession
SciLinks code: HSM1475

515

Use the Illustrations and Photos

Art shows complex ideas and processes. Learn to analyze the art so that you better understand the material you read in the text.

Tables and graphs display important information in an organized way to help you see relationships.

A picture is worth a thousand words. Look at the photographs to see relevant examples of science concepts that you are reading about.

Answer the Section Reviews

Section Reviews test your knowledge of the main points of the section. Critical Thinking items challenge you to think about the material in greater depth and to find connections that you infer from the text.

STUDY TIP When you can't answer a question, reread the section. The answer is usually there.

Do Your Homework

Your teacher may assign worksheets to help you understand and remember the material in the chapter.

STUDY TIP Don't try to answer the questions without reading the text and reviewing your class notes. A little preparation up front will make your homework assignments a lot easier. Answering the items in the Chapter Review will help prepare you for the chapter test.

Holt Online Learning

Visit Holt Online Learning

If your teacher gives you a special password to log onto the **Holt Online Learning** site, you'll find your complete textbook on the Web. In addition, you'll find some great learning tools and practice quizzes. You'll be able to see how well you know the material from your textbook.

SAFETY FIRST!

Exploring, inventing, and investigating are essential to the study of science. However, these activities can also be dangerous. To make sure that your experiments and explorations are safe, you must be aware of a variety of safety guidelines. You have probably heard of the saying, "It is better to be safe than sorry." This is particularly true in a science classroom where experiments and explorations are being performed. Being uninformed and careless can result in serious injuries. Don't take chances with your own safety or with anyone else's.

The following pages describe important guidelines for staying safe in the science classroom. Your teacher may also have safety guidelines and tips that are specific to your classroom and laboratory. Take the time to be safe.

Safety Rules!

Start Out Right

Always get your teacher's permission before attempting any laboratory exploration. Read the procedures carefully, and pay particular attention to safety information and caution statements. If you are unsure about what a safety symbol means, look it up or ask your teacher. You cannot be too careful when it comes to safety. If an accident does occur, inform your teacher immediately regardless of how minor you think the accident is.

If you are instructed to note the odor of a substance, wave the fumes toward your nose with your hand. Never put your nose close to the source.

Safety Symbols

All of the experiments and investigations in this book and their related worksheets include important safety symbols to alert you to particular safety concerns. Become familiar with these symbols so that when you see them, you will know what they mean and what to do. It is important that you read this entire safety section to learn about specific dangers in the laboratory.

Eye protection

Clothing protection

Hand safety

Heating safety

Electric safety

Chemical safety

Animal safety

Sharp object

Plant safety

Eye Safety

Wear safety goggles when working around chemicals, acids, bases, or any type of flame or heating device. Wear safety goggles any time there is even the slightest chance that harm could come to your eyes. If any substance gets into your eyes, notify your teacher immediately and flush your eyes with running water for at least 15 minutes. Treat any unknown chemical as if it were a dangerous chemical. Never look directly into the sun. Doing so could cause permanent blindness.

Avoid wearing contact lenses in a laboratory situation. Even if you are wearing safety goggles, chemicals can get between the contact lenses and your eyes. If your doctor requires that you wear contact lenses instead of glasses, wear eye-cup safety goggles in the lab.

Safety Equipment

Know the locations of the nearest fire alarms and any other safety equipment, such as fire blankets and eyewash fountains, as identified by your teacher, and know the procedures for using the equipment.

Neatness

Keep your work area free of all unnecessary books and papers. Tie back long hair, and secure loose sleeves or other loose articles of clothing, such as ties and bows. Remove dangling jewelry. Don't wear open-toed shoes or sandals in the laboratory. Never eat, drink, or apply cosmetics in a laboratory setting. Food, drink, and cosmetics can easily become contaminated with dangerous materials.

Certain hair products (such as aerosol hair spray) are flammable and should not be worn while working near an open flame. Avoid wearing hair spray or hair gel on lab days.

Sharp/Pointed Objects

Use knives and other sharp instruments with extreme care. Never cut objects while holding them in your hands. Place objects on a suitable work surface for cutting.

Be extra careful when using any glassware. When adding a heavy object to a graduated cylinder, tilt the cylinder so the object slides slowly to the bottom.

Heat

Wear safety goggles when using a heating device or a flame. Whenever possible, use an electric hot plate as a heat source instead of using an open flame. When heating materials in a test tube, always angle the test tube away from yourself and others. To avoid burns, wear heat-resistant gloves whenever instructed to do so.

Electricity

Be careful with electrical cords. When using a microscope with a lamp, do not place the cord where it could trip someone. Do not let cords hang over a table edge in a way that could cause equipment to fall if the cord is accidentally pulled. Do not use equipment with damaged cords. Be sure that your hands are dry and that the electrical equipment is in the "off" position before plugging it in. Turn off and unplug electrical equipment when you are finished.

Chemicals

Wear safety goggles when handling any potentially dangerous chemicals, acids, or bases. If a chemical is unknown, handle it as you would a dangerous chemical. Wear an apron and protective gloves when you work with acids or bases or whenever you are told to do so. If a spill gets on your skin or clothing, rinse it off immediately with water for at least 5 minutes while calling to your teacher.

Never mix chemicals unless your teacher tells you to do so. Never taste, touch, or smell chemicals unless you are specifically directed to do so. Before working with a flammable liquid or gas, check for the presence of any source of flame, spark, or heat.

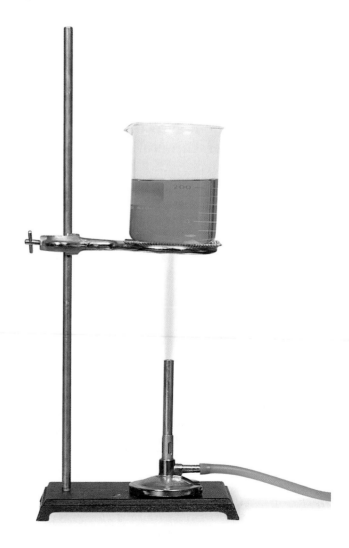

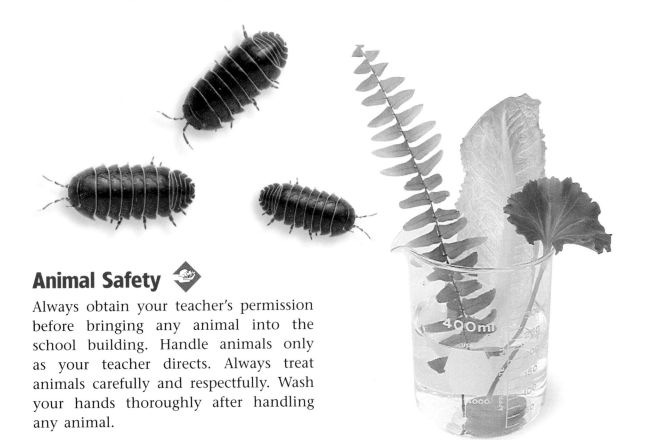

Animal Safety

Always obtain your teacher's permission before bringing any animal into the school building. Handle animals only as your teacher directs. Always treat animals carefully and respectfully. Wash your hands thoroughly after handling any animal.

Plant Safety

Do not eat any part of a plant or plant seed used in the laboratory. Wash your hands thoroughly after handling any part of a plant. When in nature, do not pick any wild plants unless your teacher instructs you to do so.

Glassware

Examine all glassware before use. Be sure that glassware is clean and free of chips and cracks. Report damaged glassware to your teacher. Glass containers used for heating should be made of heat-resistant glass.

1

Interactions of Living Things

The Big Idea

Organisms interact with each other and with the nonliving parts of their environment.

SECTION

1 Everything Is Connected 4

2 Living Things Need Energy 8

3 Types of Interactions 14

About the

A chameleon is about to grab an insect using its long tongue. A chameleon's body can change color to match its surroundings. Blending in helps the chameleon sneak up on its prey and also keeps the chameleon safe from animals that would like to make a snack out of a chameleon.

PRE-READING ACTIVITY

 **Tri-Fold** Before you read the chapter, create the FoldNote entitled "Tri-Fold" described in the **Study Skills** section of the Appendix. Write what you know about the interactions of living things in the column labeled "Know." Then, write what you want to know in the column labeled "Want." As you read the chapter, write what you learn about the interactions of living things in the column labeled "Learn."

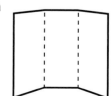

START-UP ACTIVITY

Who Eats Whom?

In this activity, you will learn how organisms interact when finding (or becoming) the next meal.

Procedure

1. On each of **five index cards,** print the name of one of the following organisms: killer whale, cod fish, krill shrimp, algae, and leopard seal.

2. On your desk, arrange the cards in a chain to show who eats whom.

3. Record the order of your cards.

4. In nature, would you expect to see more killer whales or cod? Arrange the cards in order of most individuals in an organism group to fewest.

Analysis

1. What might happen to the other organisms if algae were removed from this group? What might happen if the killer whales were removed?

2. Are there any organisms in this group that eat more than one kind of food? (Hint: What else might a seal, a fish, or a killer whale eat?) How could you change the order of your cards to show this information? How could you use pieces of string to show these relationships?

Everything Is Connected

An alligator drifts in a weedy Florida river, watching a long, thin fish called a *gar*. The gar swims too close to the alligator. Then, in a rush of murky water, the alligator swallows the gar whole and slowly swims away.

It is clear that two organisms have interacted when one eats the other. But organisms have many interactions other than simply "who eats whom." For example, alligators dig underwater holes to escape from the heat. After the alligators abandon these holes, fish and other aquatic organisms live in the holes during the winter dry period.

Studying the Web of Life

All living things are connected in a web of life. Scientists who study the web of life specialize in the science of ecology. **Ecology** is the study of the interactions of organisms with one another and with their environment.

The Two Parts of an Environment

An organism's environment consists of all the things that affect the organism. These things can be divided into two groups. All of the organisms that live together and interact with one another make up the **biotic** part of the environment. The **abiotic** part of the environment consists of the nonliving factors, such as water, soil, light, and temperature. How many biotic parts and abiotic parts do you see in **Figure 1**?

Figure 1 *The alligator affects, and is affected by, many organisms in its environment.*

Organization in the Environment

At first glance, the environment may seem disorganized. However, the environment can be arranged into different levels, as shown in **Figure 2.** The first level is made of an individual organism. The second level is larger and is made of similar organisms, which form a population. The third level is made of different populations, which form a community. The fourth level is made of a community and its abiotic environment, which form an ecosystem. The fifth and final level contains all ecosystems, which form the biosphere.

ecology the study of the interactions of living organisms with one another and with their environment

biotic describes living factors in the environment

abiotic describes the nonliving part of the environment, including water, rocks, light, and temperature

Figure 2 **The Five Levels of Environmental Organization**

Biosphere

Ecosystem

Community

Population

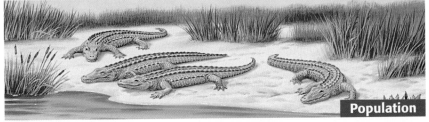

Organism

Meeting the Neighbors

1. Explore two or three blocks of your neighborhood.

2. Draw a map of the area's biotic and abiotic features. For example, map the location of sidewalks, large rocks, trees, water features, and any animals you see. Remember to approach all plants and animals with caution. Use your map to answer the following questions.

3. How are the biotic factors affected by the abiotic factors?

4. How are the abiotic factors affected by the biotic factors?

Populations

A salt marsh, such as the one shown in **Figure 3,** is a coastal area where grasslike plants grow. Within the salt marsh are animals. Each animal is a part of a **population,** or a group of individuals of the same species that live together. For example, all of the seaside sparrows that live in the same salt marsh are members of a population. The individuals in the population often compete with one another for food, nesting space, and mates.

Communities

A **community** consists of all of the populations of species that live and interact in an area. The animals and plants you see in **Figure 3** form a salt-marsh community. The populations in a community depend on each other for food, shelter, and many other things.

population a group of organisms of the same species that live in a specific geographical area

community all the populations of species that live in the same habitat and interact with each other

Figure 3 *Examine the picture of a salt marsh. Try to find examples of each level of organization in this environment.*

Laughing gull

Egret

Cordgrass

Heron

Seaside sparrows eat insects, spiders, and small crabs. A male and his mate weave a nest out of cordgrass stalks.

Juvenile sea croaker

The little marsh crab eats cordgrass as well as tiny shrimp.

Jellyfish

Some animals eat cordgrass, along with the microscopic algae that grow on the surface of its leaves and stems.

The periwinkle snail eats the algae that grow on the cordgrass. The periwinkle snail also uses the cordgrass as a place to hide from predators.

Ecosystems

An **ecosystem** is made up of a community of organisms and the abiotic environment of the community. An ecologist studying the ecosystem could examine how organisms interact as well as how temperature, precipitation, and soil characteristics affect the organisms. For example, the rivers that empty into the salt marsh carry nutrients, such as nitrogen, from the land. These nutrients affect the growth of the cordgrass and algae.

The Biosphere

The **biosphere** is the part of Earth where life exists. It extends from the deepest parts of the ocean to high in the air where plant spores drift. Ecologists study the biosphere to learn how organisms interact with the abiotic environment—Earth's atmosphere, water, soil, and rock. The water in the abiotic environment includes fresh water and salt water as well as water that is frozen in polar icecaps and glaciers.

✓ **Reading Check** What is the biosphere? (*See the Appendix for answers to Reading Checks.*)

ecosystem a community of organisms and their abiotic environment

biosphere the part of Earth where life exists

INTERNET ACTIVITY

For another activity related to this chapter, go to **go.hrw.com** and type in the keyword **HL5INTW**.

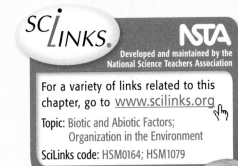

SECTION Review

Summary

- All living things are connected in a web of life.
- The biotic part of an environment is made up of all of the living things found within it.
- The abiotic part of an environment is made up of all of the nonliving things found within it, such as water and light.
- An ecosystem is made up of a community of organisms and its abiotic environment.

Using Key Terms

1. In your own words, write a definition for the term *ecology*.

2. Use the following terms in the same sentence: *biotic* and *abiotic*.

Understanding Key Ideas

3. Which one of the following is the highest level of environmental organization?

   a. ecosystem   **c.** population
   b. community   **d.** organism

4. What makes up a community?

5. Give two examples of how abiotic factors can affect an ecosystem.

Math Skills

6. From sea level, the biosphere goes up about 9 km and down about 19 km. What is the thickness of the biosphere in meters?

Critical Thinking

7. **Analyzing Relationships** What would happen to the other organisms in the salt-marsh ecosystem if the cordgrass suddenly died?

8. **Identifying Relationships** Explain in your own words what people mean when they say that everything is connected.

9. **Analyzing Ideas** Do ecosystems have borders? Explain your answer.

SCILINKS

NSTA
Developed and maintained by the National Science Teachers Association

For a variety of links related to this chapter, go to www.scilinks.org

Topic: Biotic and Abiotic Factors; Organization in the Environment
SciLinks code: HSM0164; HSM1079

Living Things Need Energy

Do you think you could survive on only water and vitamins? Eating food satisfies your hunger because it provides something you cannot live without—energy.

Living things need energy to survive. For example, black-tailed prairie dogs, which live in the grasslands of North America, eat grass and seeds to get the energy they need. Everything a prairie dog does requires energy. The same is true for the plants that grow in the grasslands where the prairie dogs live.

The Energy Connection

Organisms, in a prairie or any community, can be divided into three groups based on how they get energy. These groups are producers, consumers, and decomposers. Examine **Figure 1** to see how energy passes through an ecosystem.

Producers

Organisms that use sunlight directly to make food are called *producers*. They do this by using a process called *photosynthesis*. Most producers are plants, but algae and some bacteria are also producers. Grasses are the main producers in a prairie ecosystem. Examples of producers in other ecosystems include cordgrass and algae in a salt marsh and trees in a forest. Algae are the main producers in the ocean.

What You Will Learn

● Describe the functions of producers, consumers, and decomposers in an ecosystem.
● Distinguish between a food chain and a food web.
● Explain how energy flows through a food web.
● Describe how the removal of one species affects the entire food web.

Vocabulary

herbivore   food chain
carnivore   food web
omnivore   energy pyramid

READING STRATEGY

Reading Organizer As you read this section, make a table comparing producers, consumers, and decomposers.

Figure 1 *Living things get their energy either from the sun or from eating other organisms.*

Energy Sunlight is the source of energy for almost all living things.

Producer Plants use the energy in sunlight to make food.

Consumer The black-tailed prairie dog (herbivore) eats seeds and grass in the grasslands of western North America.

Consumer All of the prairie dogs in a colony watch for enemies, such as coyotes (carnivore), hawks, and badgers. Occasionally, a prairie dog is killed and eaten by a coyote.

Consumers

Organisms that eat other organisms are called *consumers*. They cannot use the sun's energy to make food like producers can. Instead, consumers eat producers or other animals to obtain energy. There are several kinds of consumers. A consumer that eats only plants is called a **herbivore.** Herbivores found in the prairie include grasshoppers, prairie dogs, and bison. A **carnivore** is a consumer that eats animals. Carnivores in the prairie include coyotes, hawks, badgers, and owls. Consumers known as **omnivores** eat both plants and animals. The grasshopper mouse is an example of an omnivore. It eats insects, lizards, and grass seeds.

Scavengers are omnivores that eat dead plants and animals. The turkey vulture is a scavenger in the prairie. A vulture will eat what is left after a coyote has killed and eaten an animal. Scavengers also eat animals and plants that have died from natural causes.

✔ **Reading Check** **What are organisms that eat other organisms called?** (*See the Appendix for answers to Reading Checks.*)

Decomposers

Organisms that get energy by breaking down dead organisms are called *decomposers*. Bacteria and fungi are decomposers. These organisms remove stored energy from dead organisms. They produce simple materials, such as water and carbon dioxide, which can be used by other living things. Decomposers are important because they are nature's recyclers.

herbivore an organism that eats only plants

carnivore an organism that eats animals

omnivore an organism that eats both plants and animals

A Chain Game

With the help of your parent, make a list of the foods you ate at your most recent meal. Trace the energy of each food back to the sun. Which foods on your list were consumers? How many were producers?

Consumer A turkey vulture (scavenger) may eat some of the coyote's leftovers. A scavenger can pick bones completely clean.

Decomposer Any prairie dog remains not eaten by the coyote or the turkey vulture are broken down by bacteria (decomposer) and fungi that live in the soil.

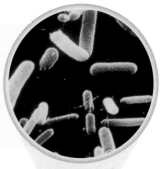

Food Chains and Food Webs

food chain the pathway of energy transfer through various stages as a result of the feeding patterns of a series of organisms

food web a diagram that shows the feeding relationships between organisms in an ecosystem

Figure 1 on the previous page, shows a food chain. A **food chain** is a diagram that shows how energy in food flows from one organism to another. Because few organisms eat just one kind of food, simple food chains are rare.

The energy connections in nature are more accurately shown by a food web than by a food chain. A **food web** is a diagram that shows the feeding relationships between organisms in an ecosystem. **Figure 2** shows a simple food web. Notice that an arrow goes from the prairie dog to the coyote, showing that the prairie dog is food for the coyote. The prairie dog is also food for the mountain lion. Energy moves from one organism to the next in a one-way direction, even in a food web. Any energy not immediately used by an organism is stored in its tissues. Only the energy stored in an organism's tissues can be used by the next consumer. There are two main food webs on Earth: a land food web and an aquatic food web.

Figure 2 *The green arrows show how energy moves when one organism eats another. Most consumers eat a variety of foods and can be eaten by a variety of other consumers.*

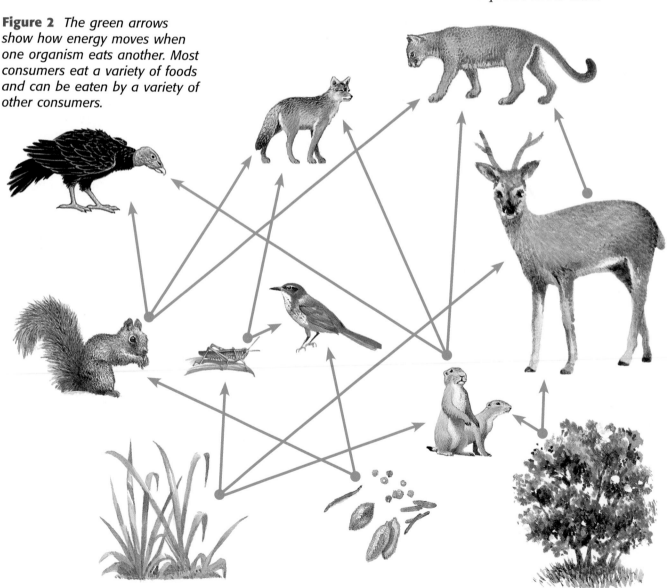

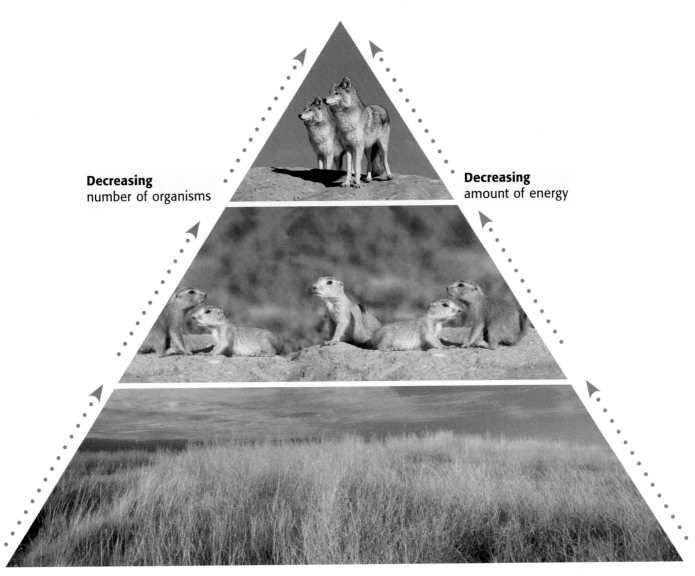

Decreasing number of organisms

Decreasing amount of energy

Figure 3 *The pyramid represents energy. As you can see, more energy is available at the base of the pyramid than at its top.*

Energy Pyramids

Grass uses most of the energy it gets from sunlight for its own life processes. But some of the energy is stored in the grass' tissues. This energy is used by the prairie dogs and other animals that eat the grass. Prairie dogs use most of the energy they get from eating grass and store only a little in their tissues. Therefore, a population of prairie dogs can support only a few coyotes. In the community, there must be more grass than prairie dogs and more prairie dogs than coyotes.

The energy at each level of the food chain can be seen in an energy pyramid. An **energy pyramid** is a diagram that shows an ecosystem's loss of energy. An example of an energy pyramid is shown in **Figure 3.** You can see that the energy pyramid has a large base and a small top. Less energy is available at higher levels because only energy stored in the tissues of an organism can be transferred to the next level.

✓ Reading Check What is an energy pyramid?

energy pyramid a triangular diagram that shows an ecosystem's loss of energy, which results as energy passes through the ecosystem's food chain

Figure 4 *As the wilderness was settled, the gray wolf population in the United States declined.*

Wolves and the Energy Pyramid

One species can be very important to the flow of energy in an environment. Gray wolves, which are shown in **Figure 4,** are consumers that control the populations of many other animals. The diet of gray wolves can include anything from a lizard to an elk. Because gray wolves are predators that prey on large animals, their place is at the top of the food pyramid.

Once common throughout much of the United States, gray wolves were almost wiped out as the wilderness was settled. Without wolves, some species, such as elk, were no longer controlled. The overpopulation of elk in some areas led to overgrazing. The overgrazing left too little grass to support the elk and other populations who depended on the grass for food. Soon, almost all of the populations in the area were affected by the loss of the gray wolves.

✓ Reading Check How were other animals affected by the disappearance of the gray wolf?

Figure 5 *In small wolf packs, only one female has pups. They are cared for by all of the males and females in the pack.*

Gray Wolves and the Food Web

Gray wolves were brought back to Yellowstone National Park in 1995. The reintroduced wolves soon began to breed. **Figure 5** shows a wolf caring for pups. The U.S. Fish and Wildlife Service thinks the return of the wolves will restore the natural energy flow in the area, bring populations back into balance, and help restore the park's natural integrity.

Not everyone approves, however. Ranchers near Yellowstone are concerned about the safety of their livestock. Cows and sheep are not the natural prey of wolves. However, the wolves will eat cows and sheep if they are given the chance.

Balance in Ecosystems

As wolves become reestablished in Yellowstone National Park, they kill the old, injured, and diseased elk. This process is reducing the number of elk. The smaller elk population is letting more plants grow. So, the numbers of animals that eat the plants, such as snowshoe hares, and the animals that eat the hares, such as foxes, are increasing.

All organisms in a food web are important for the health and balance of all other organisms in the food web. But the debate over the introduction of wolves to Yellowstone National Park will most likely continue for years to come.

Energy Pyramids

Draw an energy pyramid for a river ecosystem that contains four levels—aquatic plants, insect larvae, bluegill fish, and a largemouth bass. The plants obtain 10,000 units of energy from sunlight. If each level uses 90% of the energy it receives from the previous level, how many units of energy are available to the bass?

SECTION
Review

Summary

- Producers use the energy in sunlight to make their own food.
- Consumers eat producers and other organisms to gain energy.
- Food chains represent how energy flows from one organism to another.
- All organisms are important to maintain the balance of energy in the food web.
- Energy pyramids show how energy is lost at each food chain level.

Using Key Terms

1. Use each of the following terms in a separate sentence: *herbivores, carnivores,* and *omnivores*.

2. In your own words, write a definition for each of the following terms: *food chain, food web,* and *energy pyramid*.

Understanding Key Ideas

3. Herbivores, carnivores, and scavengers are all examples of
   a. producers.   **c.** consumers.
   b. decomposers. **d.** omnivores.

4. Explain the importance of decomposers in an ecosystem.

5. Describe how producers, consumers, and decomposers are linked in a food chain.

6. Describe how energy flows through a food web.

Math Skills

7. The plants in each square meter of an ecosystem obtained 20,810 Calories of energy from sunlight per year. The herbivores in that ecosystem ate all the plants but obtained only 3,370 Calories of energy. How much energy did the plants use?

Critical Thinking

8. **Identifying Relationships** Draw two food chains, and depict how they link together to form a food web.

9. **Applying Concepts** Are consumers found at the top or bottom of an energy pyramid? Explain your answer.

10. **Predicting Consequences** What would happen if a species disappeared from an ecosystem?

For a variety of links related to this chapter, go to www.scilinks.org

Topic: Food Chains and Food Webs
SciLinks code: HSM0594

13

Types of Interactions

Look at the seaweed forest shown in **Figure 1** below. How many fish do you see? How many seaweed plants do you count? Why do you think there are more members of the seaweed population than members of the fish population?

In natural communities, the sizes of populations of different organisms can vary greatly. This variation happens because everything in the environment affects every other thing. Populations also affect every other population.

Interactions with the Environment

Most living things produce more offspring than will survive. A female frog, for example, might lay hundreds of eggs in a small pond. In a few months, the population of frogs in that pond will be about the same as it was the year before. Why won't the pond become overrun with frogs? An organism, such as a frog, interacts with biotic and abiotic factors in its environment that can control the size of its population.

Limiting Factors

Populations cannot grow without stopping, because the environment contains a limited amount of food, water, living space, and other resources. A resource that is so scarce that it limits the size of a population is called a *limiting factor*. For example, food becomes a limiting factor when a population becomes too large for the amount of food available. Any single resource can be a limiting factor to a population's size.

What You Will Learn

- Explain the relationship between carrying capacity and limiting factors.
- Describe the two types of competition.
- Distinguish between mutualism, commensalism, and parasitism. Give an example of coevolution.

Vocabulary

carrying capacity   mutualism
prey   commensalism
predator   parasitism
symbiosis   coevolution

READING STRATEGY

Reading Organizer As you read this section, make a concept map by using the terms above.

Figure 1 *This seaweed forest is home to a large number of interacting species.*

Carrying Capacity

The largest population that an environment can support is known as the **carrying capacity.** When a population grows larger than its carrying capacity, limiting factors in the environment cause individuals to die off or leave. As individuals die or leave, the population decreases.

For example, after a rainy season, plants may produce a large crop of leaves and seeds. This large amount of food may cause an herbivore population to grow. If the next year has less rainfall, there won't be enough food to support the large herbivore population. In this way, a population may become larger than the carrying capacity, but only for a little while. A limiting factor will cause the population to die back. The population will return to a size that the environment can support.

carrying capacity the largest population that an environment can support at any given time

Interactions Between Organisms

Populations contain individuals of a single species that interact with one another, such as a group of rabbits feeding in the same area. Communities contain interacting populations, such as a coral reef with many species of corals trying to find living space. Ecologists have described four main ways that species and individuals affect each other: competition, predators and prey, symbiotic relationships, and coevolution.

Reading Check **What are four main ways organisms affect one another?** (*See the Appendix for answers to Reading Checks.*)

Competition

When two or more individuals or populations try to use the same resource, such as food, water, shelter, space, or sunlight, it is called *competition*. Because resources are in limited supply in the environment, their use by one individual or population decreases the amount available to other organisms.

Competition happens between individuals *within* a population. The elks in Yellowstone National Park are herbivores that compete with each other for the same food plants in the park. This competition is a big problem in winter when many plants die.

Competition also happens *between* populations. The different species of trees in **Figure 2** are competing with each other for sunlight and space.

Figure 2 *Some of the trees in this forest grow tall to reach sunlight, which reduces the amount of sunlight available to shorter trees nearby.*

Predators and Prey

Many interactions between species consist of one organism eating another. The organism that is eaten is called the **prey.** The organism that eats the prey is called the **predator.** When a bird eats a worm, the worm is prey and the bird is the predator.

Predator Adaptations

To survive, predators must be able to catch their prey. Predators have a wide variety of methods and abilities for doing so. The cheetah, for example, is able to run very quickly to catch its prey. The cheetah's speed gives it an advantage over other predators competing for the same prey.

Other predators, such as the goldenrod spider, shown in **Figure 3,** ambush their prey. The goldenrod spider blends in so well with the goldenrod flower that all it has to do is wait for its next insect meal to arrive.

Prey Adaptations

Prey have their own methods and abilities to keep from being eaten. Prey are able to run away, stay in groups, or camouflage themselves. Some prey are poisonous. They may advertise their poison with bright colors to warn predators to stay away. The fire salamander, shown in **Figure 4,** sprays a poison that burns. Predators quickly learn to recognize its *warning coloration.*

Many animals run away from predators. Prairie dogs run to their underground burrows when a predator approaches. Many small fishes, such as anchovies, swim in groups called *schools.* Antelopes and buffaloes stay in herds. All the eyes, ears, and noses of the individuals in the group are watching, listening, and smelling for predators. This behavior increases the likelihood of spotting a potential predator.

prey an organism that is killed and eaten by another organism

predator an organism that eats all or part of another organism

Figure 3 *The goldenrod spider is difficult for its insect prey to see. Can you see it?*

Figure 4 *Many predators know better than to eat the fire salamander! This colorful animal will make a predator very sick.*

Camouflage

One way animals avoid being eaten is by being hard to see. A rabbit often freezes so that its natural color blends into a background of shrubs or grass. Blending in with the background is called *camouflage*. Many animals mimic twigs, leaves, stones, bark, or other materials in their environment. One insect, called a walking stick, looks just like a twig. Some walking sticks even sway a bit, as though a breeze were blowing.

Reading Check What is camouflage, and how does it prevent an animal from being eaten?

Defensive Chemicals

The spines of a porcupine clearly signal trouble to a potential predator, but other defenses may not be as obvious. Some animals defend themselves with chemicals. The skunk and the bombardier beetle both spray predators with irritating chemicals. Bees, ants, and wasps inject a powerful acid into their attackers. The skin of both the poison arrow frog and a bird called the *hooded pitohui* contains a deadly toxin. Any predator that eats, or tries to eat, one of these animals will likely die.

Warning Coloration

Animals that have a chemical defense need a way to warn predators that they should look elsewhere for a meal. Their chemical weapons are often advertised by warning colors, as shown in **Figure 5.** Predators will avoid any animal that has the colors and patterns they associate with pain, illness, or unpleasant experiences. The most common warning colors are bright shades of red, yellow, orange, black, and white.

CONNECTION TO Environmental Science

Pretenders Some animals are pretenders. They don't have defensive chemicals. But they use warning coloration to their advantage. The Scarlet king snake has colored stripes that make it look like the poisonous coral snake. Even though the Scarlet king snake is harmless, predators see its bright colors and leave it alone. What might happen if there were more pretenders than there were animals with real defensive chemicals?

Figure 5 *The warning coloration of the yellow jacket (left) and the pitohui (above) warns predators that they are dangerous.*

Symbiosis

Some species have very close interactions with other species. **Symbiosis** is a close, long-term association between two or more species. The individuals in a symbiotic relationship can benefit from, be unaffected by, or be harmed by the relationship. Often, one species lives in or on the other species. The thousands of symbiotic relationships in nature are often classified into three groups: mutualism, commensalism, and parasitism.

symbiosis a relationship in which two different organisms live in close association with each other

mutualism a relationship between two species in which both species benefit

commensalism a relationship between two organisms in which one organism benefits and the other is unaffected

Mutualism

A symbiotic relationship in which both organisms benefit is called **mutualism** (MYOO choo uhl ɪz uhm). For example, you and a species of bacteria that lives in your intestines benefit each other! The bacteria get food from you, and you get vitamins that the bacteria produce.

Mutualism also occurs between some corals and the algae living inside those corals. In this relationship, a coral receives the extra food that the algae make by photosynthesis. In turn, these algae also receive a place to live, as **Figure 6** shows. These algae also receive some nutrients from the coral. Both organisms benefit from this relationship.

Figure 6 *In the smaller photo above, you can see the gold-colored algae inside the coral.*

✔ *Reading Check* **Which organism benefits in mutualism?**

Commensalism

A symbiotic relationship in which one organism benefits and the other is unaffected is called **commensalism.** One example of commensalism is the relationship between sharks and smaller fish called *remoras*. **Figure 7** shows a shark with a remora attached to its body. Remoras "hitch a ride" and feed on scraps of food left by sharks. The remoras benefit from this relationship, while sharks are unaffected.

Figure 7 *The remora attached to the shark benefits from the relationship. The shark neither benefits from nor is harmed by the relationship.*

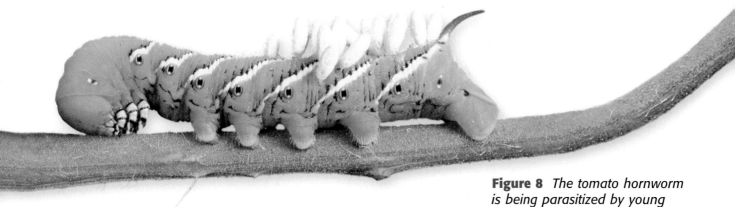

Parasitism

A symbiotic association in which one organism benefits while the other is harmed is called **parasitism** (PAR uh SIT iz uhm). The organism that benefits is called the *parasite*. The organism that is harmed is called the *host*. The parasite gets nourishment from its host while the host is weakened. Sometimes, a host dies. Parasites, such as ticks, live outside the host's body. Other parasites, such as tapeworms, live inside the host's body.

Figure 8 shows a bright green caterpillar called a *tomato hornworm*. A female wasp laid tiny eggs on the caterpillar. When the eggs hatch, each young wasp will burrow into the caterpillar's body. The young wasps will actually eat the caterpillar alive! In a short time, the caterpillar will be almost completely eaten and will die. When that happens, the adult wasps will fly away.

In this example of parasitism, the host dies. Most parasites, however, do not kill their hosts. Most parasites don't kill their hosts because parasites depend on their hosts. If a parasite were to kill its host, the parasite would have to find a new host.

parasitism a relationship between two species in which one species, the parasite, benefits from the other species, the host, which is harmed

coevolution the evolution of two species that is due to mutual influence, often in a way that makes the relationship more beneficial to both species

Coevolution

Relationships between organisms change over time. Interactions can also change the organisms themselves. When a long-term change takes place in two species because of their close interactions with one another, the change is called **coevolution.**

The ant and the acacia tree shown in **Figure 9** have a mutualistic relationship. The ants protect the tree by attacking other organisms that come near the tree. The tree has special structures that make food for the ants. The ants and the acacia tree may have coevolved through interactions between the two species. Coevolution can take place between any organisms that live close together. But changes happen over a very long period of time.

Figure 9 *Ants collect food made by the acacia tree and store the food in their shelter, which is also made by the tree.*

Rabbits in Australia In 1859, settlers released 12 rabbits in Australia. There was plenty of food and no natural predators for the rabbits. The rabbit population increased so fast that the country was soon overrun by rabbits. Then, the Australian government introduced a rabbit virus to control the population. The first time the virus was used, more than 99% of the rabbits died. The survivors reproduced, and the rabbit population grew large again. The second time the virus was used, about 90% of the rabbits died. Once again, the rabbit population increased. The third time the virus was used, only about 50% of the rabbits died. Suggest what changes might have occurred in the rabbits and the virus.

Coevolution and Flowers

A *pollinator* is an organism that carries pollen from one flower to another. Pollination is necessary for reproduction in most plants.

Flowers have changed over millions of years to attract pollinators. Pollinators such as bees, bats, and hummingbirds can be attracted to a flower because of its color, odor, or nectar. Flowers pollinated by hummingbirds make nectar with the right amount of sugar for the bird. Hummingbirds have long beaks, which help them drink the nectar.

Some bats, such as the one shown in **Figure 10,** changed over time to have long, thin tongues and noses to help them reach the nectar in flowers. As the bat feeds on the nectar, its nose becomes covered with pollen. The next flower it eats from will be pollinated with the pollen it is gathering from this flower. The long nose helps it to feed and also makes it a better pollinator.

Because flowers and their pollinators have interacted so closely over millions of years, there are many examples of coevolution between them.

☑ Reading Check Why do flowers need to attract pollinators?

Figure 10 *This bat is drinking nectar with its long, skinny tongue. The bat has coevolved with the flower over millions of years.*

Summary

- Limiting factors in the environment keep a population from growing without limit.
- Two or more individuals or populations trying to use the same resource is called *competition.*
- A predator is an organism that eats all or part of another organism. The organism that is eaten is called *prey.*

- Prey have developed features such as camouflage, chemical defenses, and warning coloration, to protect them from predators.
- Symbiosis occurs when two organisms form a very close relationship with one another over time.
- Close relationships over a very long time can result in coevolution. For example, flowers and their pollinators have evolved traits that benefit both.

Using Key Terms

1. In your own words, write a definition for the term *carrying capacity.*

2. Use each of the following terms in a separate sentence: *mutualism, commensalism,* and *parasitism.*

Understanding Key Ideas

3. Which of the following is NOT a prey adaptation?
   a. camouflage
   b. chemical defenses
   c. warning coloration
   d. parasitism

4. Identify two things organisms compete with one another for.

5. Briefly describe one example of a predator-prey relationship. Identify the predator and the prey.

Critical Thinking

6. **Making Comparisons** Compare coevolution with symbiosis.

7. **Identifying Relationships** Explain the probable relationship between the giant *Rafflesia* flower, which smells like rotting meat, and the carrion flies that buzz around it. (Hint: *Carrion* means "rotting flesh.")

8. **Predicting Consequences** Predict what might happen if all of the ants were removed from an acacia tree.

Interpreting Graphics

The population graph below shows the growth of a species of *Paramecium* (single-celled microorganism) over 18 days. Food was added to the test tube occasionally. Use this graph to answer the questions that follow.

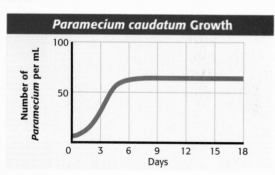

9. What is the carrying capacity of the test tube as long as food is added?

10. Predict what will happen if no more food is added?

11. What keeps the number of *Paramecium* at a steady level?

For a variety of links related to this chapter, go to www.scilinks.org

Topic: Predator/Prey; Coevolution
SciLinks code: HSM1205; HSM0309

Skills Practice Lab

Capturing the Wild Bean

OBJECTIVES

Estimate the size of a "population" of beans.

Calculate the difference between your estimation and the actual number of beans.

MATERIALS

- bag, paper lunch, small
- beans, pinto
- calculator (optional)
- marker, permanent

When wildlife biologists study a group of organisms in an area, they need to know how many organisms live there. Sometimes, biologists worry that a certain organism is outgrowing the environment's carrying capacity. Other times, scientists need to know if an organism is becoming rare so that steps can be taken to protect it. However, animals can be difficult to count because they can move around and hide. Because of this challenge, biologists have developed methods to estimate the number of animals in a specific area. One of these counting methods is called the *mark-recapture method*.

In this activity, you will enter the territory of the wild pinto bean to estimate the number of beans that live in the paper-bag habitat.

Procedure

1. Prepare a data table like the one below.

Mark-Recapture Data Table				
Number of animals in first capture	Total number of animals in recapture	Number of marked animals in recapture	Calculated estimate of population	Actual total population
	DO NOT WRITE IN BOOK			

2. Your teacher will provide you with a paper bag containing an unknown number of beans. Carefully reach into the bag, and remove a handful of beans.

3 Count the number of beans you have "captured." Record this number in your data table under "Number of animals in first capture."

4 Use the permanent marker to carefully mark each bean that you have just counted. Allow the marks to dry completely. When all the marks are dry, place the marked beans back into the bag.

5 Gently mix the beans in the bag so that the marks won't rub off. Once again, reach into the bag. "Capture" and remove a handful of beans.

6 Count the number of beans in your "recapture." Record this number in your data table under "Total number of animals in recapture."

7 Count the beans in your recapture that have marks from the first capture. Record this number in your data table under "Number of marked animals in recapture."

8 Calculate your estimation of the total number of beans in the bag by using the following equation:

$$\frac{\text{number of beans in recapture} \times \text{number of beans marked}}{\text{number of marked beans in recapture}} = \text{calculated estimate of population}$$

Enter this number in your data table under "Calculated estimate of population."

9 Place all the beans in the bag. Then empty the bag on your work table. Be careful that no beans escape! Count each bean as you place them one at a time back into the bag. Record the number in your data table under "Actual total population."

Analyze the Results

1 **Evaluating Results** How close was your estimate to the actual number of beans?

Draw Conclusions

2 **Evaluating Methods** If your estimate was not close to the actual number of beans, how might you change your mark-recapture procedure? If you did not recapture any marked beans, what might be the cause?

Applying Your Data

How could you use the mark-recapture method to estimate the population of turtles in a small pond? Explain your procedure.

Chapter Review

USING KEY TERMS

1 Use each of the following terms in a separate sentence: *symbiosis, mutualism, commensalism,* and *parasitism.*

Complete each of the following sentences by choosing the correct term from the word bank.

biotic   abiotic
ecosystem   community

2 The environment includes _____ factors including water, rocks, and light.

3 The environment also includes _____, or living, factors.

4 A community of organisms and their environment is called a(n) _____.

For each pair of terms, explain how the meanings of the terms differ.

5 *community* and *population*

6 *ecosystem* and *biosphere*

7 *producers* and *consumers*

UNDERSTANDING KEY IDEAS

Multiple Choice

8 A tick sucks blood from a dog. In this relationship, the tick is the _____ and the dog is the _____.
- **a.** parasite, prey
- **b.** predator, host
- **c.** parasite, host
- **d.** host, parasite

9 Resources such as water, food, or sunlight are likely to be limiting factors
- **a.** when population size is decreasing.
- **b.** when predators eat their prey.
- **c.** when the population is small.
- **d.** when a population is approaching the carrying capacity.

10 Nature's recyclers are
- **a.** predators.
- **b.** decomposers.
- **c.** producers.
- **d.** omnivores.

11 A beneficial association between coral and algae is an example of
- **a.** commensalism.
- **b.** parasitism.
- **c.** mutualism.
- **d.** predation.

12 The process by which energy moves through an ecosystem can be represented by
- **a.** food chains.
- **b.** energy pyramids.
- **c.** food webs.
- **d.** All of the above

13 Which organisms does the base of an energy pyramid represent?
- **a.** producers
- **b.** carnivores
- **c.** herbivores
- **d.** scavengers

14 Which of the following is the correct order in a food chain?
- **a.** sun→producers→herbivores→scavengers→carnivores
- **b.** sun→consumers→predators→parasites→hosts
- **c.** sun→producers→decomposers→consumers→omnivores
- **d.** sun→producers→herbivores→carnivores→scavengers

15 Remoras and sharks have a relationship that is best described as

a. mutualism.   **c.** predator and prey.
b. commensalism. **d.** parasitism.

Short Answer

16 Describe how energy flows through a food web.

17 Explain how the food web changed when the gray wolf disappeared from Yellowstone National Park.

18 How are the competition between two trees of the same species and the competition between two different species of trees similiar?

19 How do limiting factors affect the carrying capacity of an environment?

20 What is coevolution?

CRITICAL THINKING

21 **Concept Mapping** Use the following terms to create a concept map: *herbivores, organisms, producers, populations, ecosystems, consumers, communities, carnivores,* and *biosphere.*

22 **Identifying Relationships** Could a balanced ecosystem contain producers and consumers but not decomposers? Why or why not?

23 **Predicting Consequences** Some biologists think that certain species, such as alligators and wolves, help maintain biological diversity in their ecosystems. Predict what might happen to other organisms, such as gar fish or herons, if alligators were to become extinct in the Florida Everglades.

24 **Expressing Opinions** Do you think there is a carrying capacity for humans? Why or why not?

INTERPRETING GRAPHICS

Use the energy pyramid below to answer the questions that follow.

25 According to the energy pyramid, are there more prairie dogs or plants?

26 What level has the most energy?

27 Would an energy pyramid such as this one exist in nature?

28 How could you change this pyramid to look like one representing a real ecosystem?

Standardized Test Preparation

Read each of the passages below. Then, answer the questions that follow each passage.

Passage 1 Two or more individuals trying to use the same resource, such as food, water, shelter, space, or sunlight is called *competition*. Because resources are in limited supply in the environment, the use of them by one individual or population decreases the amount available to other organisms. Competition also occurs between individuals within a population. The elk in Yellowstone National Park are herbivores that compete with each other for the same food plants in the park.

1. According to the passage, competition occurs between which of the following?

  A individuals trying to use the same resource

  B elk and carnivores

  C food and shelter

  D individuals trying to use different resources

2. According to the passage, food, water, shelter, space, and sunlight are examples of

  F populations.

  G things found in Yellowstone National Park.

  H competition.

  I resources.

3. Based on the passage, which of the following statements is a fact?

  A Competition occurs only between individuals of different populations.

  B Competition occurs between individuals within a population and between individuals of different populations.

  C Competition increases the amount of resources available to individuals.

  D Because resources are abundant in the environment, competition rarely happens between individuals of different populations.

Passage 2 In the deserts of northern Africa and the Middle East, water is a scarce and valuable resource. In this area, no permanent streams flow except for the Nile. More than 1.6 million square kilometers of this region typically have no rainfall for years at a time. However, much of this area has large aquifers. The water that these aquifers contain dates back to much wetter times thousands of years ago. Occasionally, water reaches the surface to form an oasis. Wells supply the rest of the water used throughout the region. In some regions of Saudi Arabia and Kuwait, wells drilled for water more often strike oil.

1. According to the passage, an aquifer contains what resource?

  A oil

  B water

  C wells

  D oasis

2. Based on the passage, which of the following statements is a fact?

  F The Nile no longer flows through northern Africa and the Middle East.

  G The water found in aquifers is from recent rainfall.

  H Wells drilled in Saudi Arabia and Kuwait are more likely to strike oil than water.

  I The desert regions of northern Africa and the Middle East receive rainfall almost every day.

3. According to the passage, an oasis forms under what conditions?

  A when water stays beneath the surface

  B when water is drilled from a well

  C when it rains

  D when water reaches the surface

The graphs below show the population growth for two populations. Use these graphs to answer the questions that follow.

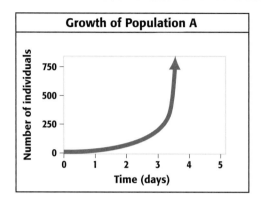

Growth of Population A

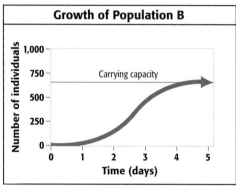

Growth of Population B

1. After 2 days, which population has more individuals?

   A Population A has more individuals.

   B Population B has more individuals.

   C The populations are the same.

   D There is not enough information to determine the answer.

2. After 5 days, which population has more individuals?

   F Population A has more individuals.

   G Population B has more individuals.

   H The populations are the same.

   I There is not enough information to determine the answer.

3. On day 10, which statement is probably true?

   A Population B is larger than population A.

   B Population A is the same as it was on day 5.

   C Population A and B are the same.

   D Population B is the same as it was on day 5.

Read each question below, and choose the best answer.

1. The figure below is a map of a forest ecosystem. What is the area of this ecosystem?

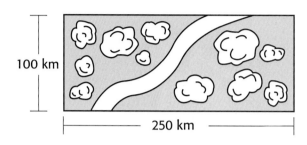

   A 25,000 km²

   B 32,000 km

   C 1,200 km²

   D 2,500 km

2. If an antelope eats 7 kg of vegetation in 2 days, how many kilograms of vegetation does it eat per day?

   F 2/7 kg

   G 3/5 kg

   H 3 1/2 kg

   I 7 1/2 kg

3. If $x = 3$ and $y = x + 2$, what is y?

   A 2

   B 4

   C 5

   D 8

4. If $x = 4$ and $y = x + 2$, what is y?

   F 2

   G 5

   H 6

   I 8

Standardized Test Preparation

Science in Action

Scientific Debate

How Did Dogs Become Pets?

Did humans change dogs to be the social and helpful creatures they are today? Or were dogs naturally social? Did dogs start moving closer to our campfires long ago? Or did humans find dogs and bring them into our homes? The way in which dogs became our friends, companions, and helpers is still a question. Some scientists think humans and training are the reasons for many of our dogs' best features. Other scientists think dogs and humans have both changed over time to form their strong and unique bond.

Math ACTIVITY

Scientists have found fossils of dogs that are 15,000 years old. Generation time is the time between the birth of one generation and the next. If the generation time for dogs is 1.5 years, how many generations have there been in the last 15,000 years?

Weird Science

Follicle Mites

What has a tiny tubelike body and short stumpy legs and lives in your eyebrows and eyelashes? Would you believe a small animal lives there? It's called a follicle mite, and humans are its host. Studies show that more than 97% of adults have these mites. Except in rare cases, follicle mites are harmless.

Like all large animals, human beings are hosts to a variety of smaller creatures that live in or on our bodies and share our bodies' resources. Bacteria that live in the lower digestive tract help to produce vitamins such as folic acid and vitamin K. Other bacteria may help maintain proper pH levels in our bodies.

Language Arts ACTIVITY

WRITING SKILL Imagine that you were shrunk to the size of a follicle mite. How would you get food? Where would you sleep? Write a short story describing one day in your new, tiny life.

Dalton Dockery

Horticulture Specialist Did you know that instead of using pesticides to get rid of insects that are eating the plants in your garden, you can use other insects? "It is a healthy way of growing vegetables without the use of chemicals and pesticides, and it reduces the harmful effects pesticides have on the environment," says Dalton Dockery, a horticulture specialist in North Carolina. Some insects, such as ladybugs and praying mantises, are natural predators of many insects that are harmful to plants. They will eat other bugs but leave your precious plants in peace. Using bugs to drive off pests is just one aspect of natural gardening. Natural gardening takes advantage of relationships that already exist in nature and uses these interactions to our benefit. For Dockery, the best parts about being a horticultural specialist are teaching people how to preserve the environment, getting to work outside regularly, and having the opportunity to help people on a daily basis.

Social Studies ACTIVITY

WRITING SKILL Research gardening or farming techniques in other cultures. Do other cultures use any of the same aspects of natural gardening as horticultural specialists? Write a short report describing your findings.

To learn more about these Science in Action topics, visit **go.hrw.com** and type in the keyword **HL5INTF.**

Current Science

Check out Current Science® articles related to this chapter by visiting **go.hrw.com.** Just type in the keyword **HL5CS18.**

2

Cycles in Nature

The Big Idea

Ecosystems change over time and depend on the cycling of matter.

SECTION

1 The Cycles of Matter 32

2 Ecological Succession 36

About the PHOTO

These penguins have a unique playground on this iceberg off the coast of Antarctica. Icebergs break off from glaciers and float out to sea. A glacier is a giant "river" of ice that slides slowly downhill. Glaciers are formed from snow piling up in mountains. Eventually, glaciers and icebergs melt and become liquid water. Water in oceans and lakes rises into the air and then falls down again as rain or snow. There is a lot of water on Earth, and most of it is constantly moving and changing form.

PRE-READING ACTIVITY

FOLDNOTES **Pyramid** Before you read the chapter, create the FoldNote entitled "Pyramid" described in the **Study Skills** section of the Appendix. Label the sides of the pyramid with "Water cycle," "Carbon cycle," and "Nitrogen cycle." As you read the chapter, define each cycle, and write the steps of each cycle on the appropriate pyramid side.

START-UP ACTIVITY

Making Rain

Do you have the power to make rain? Yes!—on a small scale. In this activity, you will cause water to change state in the same way that rain is formed. This process is one way that water is reused on Earth.

Procedure

1. Start with a **large, sealable, plastic freezer bag.** Be sure that the bag is clean and dry and has no leaks. Place a **small, dark-colored bowl** inside the bag. Position the bag with the opening at the top.

2. Fill the bowl halfway with water. Place a few drops of **red food coloring** in the water. Seal the bag.

3. Place the bowl and bag under a strong, warm **light source,** such as a lamp or direct sunlight.

4. Leave the bag in the light for as long as possible. Observe the bag at regular time intervals.

Analysis

1. Each time you observe the bag, describe what you see. Explain what you think is happening.

2. After observing the bag several times, carefully remove the bowl from the bag. Observe and describe any water that is now in the bag. Where did this water come from? How does it differ from the water in the bowl?

The Cycles of Matter

The matter in your body has been on Earth since the planet formed billions of years ago!

Matter on Earth is limited, so the matter is used over and over again. Each kind of matter has its own cycle. In these cycles, matter moves between the environment and living things.

The Water Cycle

The movement of water between the oceans, atmosphere, land, and living things is known as the *water cycle*. The parts of the water cycle are shown in **Figure 1.**

How Water Moves

During **evaporation,** the sun's heat causes water to change from liquid to vapor. In the process of **condensation,** the water vapor cools and returns to a liquid state. The water that falls from the atmosphere to the land and oceans is **precipitation.** Rain, snow, sleet, and hail are forms of precipitation. Most precipitation falls into the ocean. Some of the precipitation that falls on land flows into streams, rivers, and lakes and is called *runoff.* Some precipitation seeps into the ground and is stored in spaces between or within rocks. This water, known as *groundwater,* will slowly flow back into the soil, streams, rivers, and oceans.

What You Will Learn

- Diagram the water cycle, and explain its importance to living things.
- Diagram the carbon cycle, and explain its importance to living things.
- Diagram the nitrogen cycle, and explain its importance to living things.

Vocabulary

evaporation   decomposition
condensation   combustion
precipitation

READING STRATEGY

Mnemonics As you read this section, create a mnemonic device to help you remember the parts of the water cycle.

evaporation the change of a substance from a liquid to a gas

condensation the change of state from a gas to a liquid

precipitation any form of water that falls to the Earth's surface from the clouds

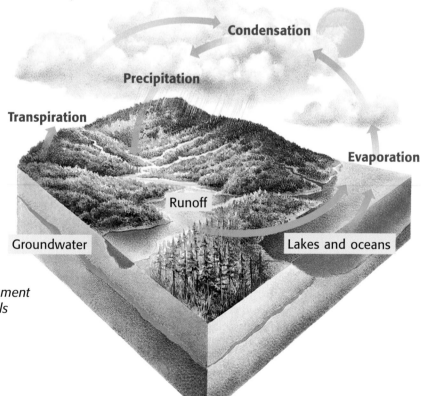

Figure 1 *Water from the environment moves through plants and animals and back to the environment.*

Short Answer

15 List four places where water can go after it falls as precipitation.

16 In what forms can water on Earth be found?

17 What role do animals have in the carbon cycle?

18 What roles do humans have in the carbon cycle?

19 Earth's atmosphere is mostly made up of what substance?

20 Compare and contrast the two forms of succession.

CRITICAL THINKING

21 **Concept Mapping** Use the following terms to create a concept map: *abandoned farmland, lichens, bare rock, soil formation, horseweed, succession, forest fire, primary succession, secondary succession,* and *pioneer species.*

22 **Identifying Relationships** Is snow a part of the water cycle? Why or why not?

23 **Analyzing Processes** Make a list of several places where water might be found on Earth. For each item on your list, state how it is part of the water cycle.

24 **Forming Hypotheses** Predict what would happen if the water on Earth suddenly stopped evaporating.

25 **Forming Hypotheses** Predict what would happen if all of the bacteria on Earth suddenly disappeared.

26 **Making Inferences** Describe why a lawn usually doesn't go through succession.

27 **Making Inferences** Can one scientist observe all of the stages of secondary succession on an abandoned field? Explain your answer.

INTERPRETING GRAPHICS

The graph below shows how water is used each day by an average household in the United States. Use the graph to answer the questions that follow.

Average Household Daily Water Use

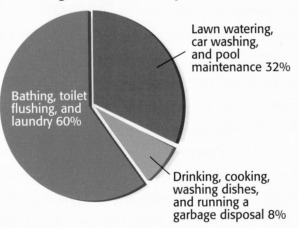

Lawn watering, car washing, and pool maintenance 32%

Bathing, toilet flushing, and laundry 60%

Drinking, cooking, washing dishes, and running a garbage disposal 8%

28 According to this graph, which of the following activities uses the greatest amount of water?

a. bathing

b. toilet flushing

c. washing laundry

d. There is not enough information to determine the answer.

29 An average family used 380 L of water per day, until they stopped washing their car, stopped watering their lawn, and stopped using their pool. Now, how much water per day do they use?

Standardized Test Preparation

Read each of the passages below. Then, answer the questions that follow each passage.

Passage 1 The scientist woke up and jogged over to the rain forest. There she observed the water-recycling experiment. She took a swim in the ocean, and she walked through the <u>aspen</u> forest on her way home. At home, she ate lunch and then went to the computer lab. From the lab, she could monitor the sensors that would alert her if any part of the ecosystem failed to cycle properly. This monitoring was very important to the scientist and her research team because their lives depended on the health of their sealed environment. Several weeks ago, the sensors began to detect trouble.

1. In the passage, what does *aspen* mean?
   A a type of experiment
   B a type of tree
   C beautiful
   D ugly

2. Based on the passage, what can the reader conclude?
   F The scientist lives in an artificial environment.
   G The scientist lives by herself.
   H The scientist and her research team are studying a newly discovered island.
   I The scientist does not rely on the sensors to detect trouble.

3. Based on the passage, which of the following statements is a fact?
   A The scientist is scared that her environment is being destroyed.
   B The scientists depend on the sensors to alert them of trouble.
   C The scientists live on an island.
   D The scientist eats lunch at home every day.

Passage 2 Every summer, millions of fish are killed in an area in the Gulf of Mexico called a *hypoxia region*. Hypoxia is a condition that occurs when there is an unusually low level of oxygen in the water. The area is often referred to as the *dead zone* because almost every fish and crustacean in the area dies. In 1995, this zone covered more than 18,000 km², and almost 1 million fish were killed in a single week. Why does this happen? Can it be stopped?

1. Based on the passage, what is the **best** definition of a hypoxia region?
   A a region where millions of fish are killed
   B a region where there is a low level of oxygen
   C a region that creates a "dead zone"
   D a region that is 18,000 km²

2. Why is the hypoxia region called a *dead zone*?
   F because the oxygen in the region is dead
   G because the region covers more area than fish can live in
   H because the Gulf of Mexico is not a popular fishing zone anymore
   I because almost every fish and crustacean in the area dies

3. What information would the paragraph following the passage provide?
   A an explanation of the definition of hypoxia
   B a description of how hypoxia occurs in other parts of the world
   C a list all of the animals that died in the Gulf of Mexico in 1995
   D an explanation of how the hypoxia region is formed in the Gulf of Mexico

The illustration below shows what an area looked like when visited on several successive occasions. Use the illustration to answer the questions that follow.

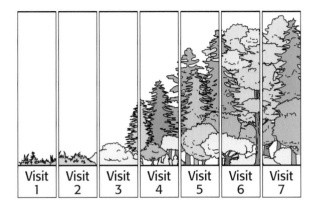

1. In the area illustrated, what process is evident over time?

   A ecological succession

   B combustion of fossil fuels

   C pioneer speciation

   D ecological organization

2. During which of the following visits would you see the **most** mature community?

   F visit 1

   G visit 3

   H visit 5

   I visit 7

3. Assume that a forest fire happened after the seventh visit. If the scientist were to visit again within 1 year after the fire, the area would most likely look like it did during which visit?

   A visit 1

   B visit 3

   C visit 5

   D visit 7

Read each question below, and choose the best answer.

1. Flushing the toilet accounts for almost half the water a person uses in a day. Some toilets use up to 6 gal per flush. More-efficient toilets use about 1.5 gal per flush. How many liters of water can you save each day by using a more-efficient toilet if you flush five times a day?

   A 4.5 gal

   B 20 gal

   C 80 L

   D 85 L

2. About 15 m of topsoil covers the eastern plains of the United States. If topsoil forms at the rate of 2.5 cm per 500 years, how long did it take for the 15 m of topsoil to form?

   F 3,000 years

   G 18,750 years

   H 30,000 years

   I 300,000 years

3. If $16 = 2x + 10$, what is x?

   A 2

   B 3

   C 4

   D 8

4. What is the area of the rectangle below?

   F 22 m

   G 22 m²

   H 105 m

   I 105 m²

Standardized Test Preparation

Science in Action

Scientific Discoveries

The Dead Zone

Every summer, millions of fish are killed in an area in the Gulf of Mexico called a hypoxia region. *Hypoxia* (hy PAWK see UH) is a condition of water with unusually low levels of oxygen. The Gulf's hypoxia region is called a "dead zone" because a large number of organisms in the area die. Why does this happen? Scientists think that the region may be polluted with large amounts of nitrogen and phosphorus. These nutrients promote the growth of algae, which "bloom" and then die in huge numbers. When the algae is decomposed by bacteria, the bacteria use up oxygen in the water and hypoxia results. Scientists think that the polluting chemicals are washed into the Gulf by the Mississippi River. This river receives runoff from a large area that includes farms, housing, and cities. The scientists propose that adding wetlands to the Mississippi River watershed could reduce the chemicals reaching the Gulf.

Science, Technology, and Society

Desalination

By the year 2025, it is estimated that almost a billion people on Earth will face water shortages. Only about 3% of the water on Earth is *fresh water*—the kind of water that we use for drinking and farming. And the human population is using and polluting Earth's fresh water too quickly. The other 97% of Earth's water is mostly in oceans and is much too salty for drinking or farming.

Until recently, it was very expensive and time-consuming to filter salt out of water, a process known as *desalination*. But new technologies are making desalination an affordable option for some areas.

Language Arts ACTIVITY

WRITING SKILL The Gulf of Mexico is not the only place where a hypoxia region exists. Research other bodies of water to find out how widespread the problem is. Write a short report telling what scientists are doing to reduce hypoxia in other places.

Math ACTIVITY

You need to drink about 2 quarts of water each day. Imagine that you have a simple device that evaporates sea water and collects fresh, drinkable water at the rate of 6 mL/min. How long will it take your device to collect enough water each day?

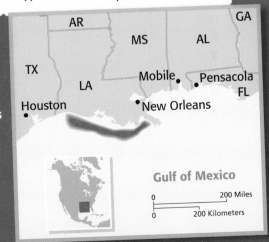

For several years after it was first noticed, the Gulf of Mexico hypoxia region became larger.

Gulf of Mexico

0 — 200 Miles
0 — 200 Kilometers

Michael Fan

Wastewater Manager If you are concerned about clean water and you like to work both in a laboratory and outdoors, you might like a career in wastewater management. The water cycle helps to keep water in nature pure enough for most organisms. But when humans use water in houses, factories, and farms, we create *wastewater*, often faster than natural processes can clean it up. To make the water safe again, we can imitate the ways water gets cleaned up in nature—and speed up the process.

Michael M. Fan is the Assistant Superintendent of wastewater operations at the Wastewater Treatment Plant at the University of California in Davis, California. This plant has one of the most advanced wastewater management systems in the country. Mr. Fan finds his job exciting. The plant operates 24 hours a day, and there are many tasks to manage. Running the plant requires skills in chemistry, physics, microbiology, and engineering. Many organisms in the Davis area are counting on Mr. Fan to make sure that the water used by the University campus is safely returned to nature.

Social Studies ACTIVITY

Research the ways that the ancient Romans managed their wastewater. Make a poster that illustrates some of their methods and technologies.

To learn more about these Science in Action topics, visit go.hrw.com and type in the keyword **HL5CYCF**

Current Science

Check out Current Science® articles related to this chapter by visiting go.hrw.com. Just type in the keyword **HL5CS19**.

3

The Earth's Ecosystems

The Big Idea

Earth's ecosystems are characterized by their living and nonliving parts.

SECTION

① Land Biomes 50

② Marine Ecosystems 58

③ Freshwater Ecosystems 64

About the PHOTO

Is this animal a movie monster? No! The thorny devil is a lizard that lives in the desert of Australia. The thorny devil's rough skin is an adaptation that helps it survive in the hot, dry desert. Grooves in the thorny devil's skin collect water that the lizard later drinks. Water lands on its back and runs along the tiny grooves to the thorny devil's mouth.

PRE-READING ACTIVITY

FOLDNOTES **Three-Panel Flip Chart**
Before you read the chapter, create the FoldNote entitled "Three-Panel Flip Chart" described in the **Study Skills** section of the Appendix. Label the flaps of the three-panel flip chart with "Land biomes," "Marine ecosystems," and "Freshwater ecosystems." As you read the chapter, write information you learn about each category under the appropriate flap.

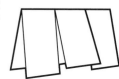

START-UP ACTIVITY

A Mini-Ecosystem

In this activity, you will build and observe a miniature ecosystem.

Procedure

1. Place a layer of **gravel** at the bottom of a **container,** such as a **large, wide-mouthed jar** or a **2 L soda bottle** with the top cut off. Then, add a layer of **soil.**

2. Add a variety of **plants** that need similar growing conditions. Choose small plants that will not grow too quickly.

3. Spray **water** inside the container to moisten the soil.

4. Loosely cover the container with a **lid** or **plastic wrap.** Place the container in indirect light.

5. Describe the appearance of your ecosystem.

6. Let your mini-ecosystem grow for 6 weeks. Add more water when the soil is dry.

7. Observe your mini-ecosystem every week. Record your observations.

Analysis

1. List the nonliving factors that make up the ecosystem that you built.

2. List the living factors that make up your ecosystem.

3. How is your mini-ecosystem similar to a real ecosystem? How is it different?

Land Biomes

What do you think of when you think of polar bears? You probably imagine them in a snow-covered setting. Why don't polar bears live in the desert?

Different ecosystems are home to different kinds of organisms. Polar bears don't live in the desert because they are adapted to very cold environments. Polar bears have thick fur. This fur keeps polar bears warm. It also hides them in the snow.

The Earth's Land Biomes

Imagine yourself in a hot, dry, dusty place. You see a cactus on your right. A lizard sits on a rock to your left. Where are you? You may not know exactly, but you probably think you are in a desert.

A desert is different from other places because of its abiotic (AY bie AHT ik) factors and biotic (bie AHT ik) factors. *Abiotic factors* are the nonliving parts of an environment. Soil, water, and climate are abiotic factors. Climate is the average weather conditions for an area over a long period of time. *Biotic factors* are the living parts of an environment. Plants and animals are biotic factors. Areas that have similar abiotic factors usually have similar biotic factors. A **biome** (BIE OHM) is a large area characterized by its climate and the plants and animals that live in the area. A biome contains related ecosystems. For example, a tropical rain forest biome contains treetop ecosystems and forest-floor ecosystems. The major land biomes on Earth are shown in **Figure 1.**

What You Will Learn

● Distinguish between abiotic factors and biotic factors in biomes.
● Identify seven land biomes on Earth.

Vocabulary

biome   desert
savanna   tundra

READING STRATEGY

Reading Organizer As you read this section, create an outline of the section. Use the headings from the section in your outline.

biome a large region characterized by a specific type of climate and certain types of plant and animal communities

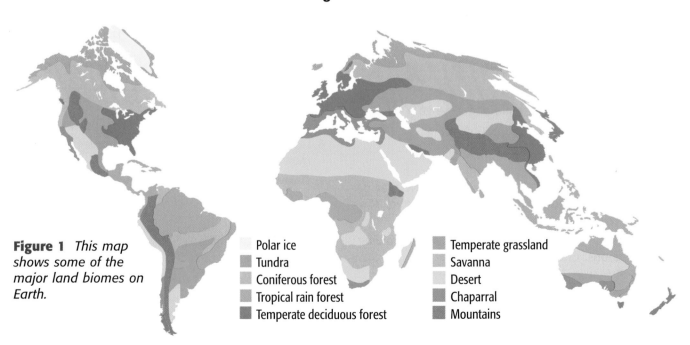

Figure 1 *This map shows some of the major land biomes on Earth.*

Polar ice	Temperate grassland
Tundra	Savanna
Coniferous forest	Desert
Tropical rain forest	Chaparral
Temperate deciduous forest	Mountains

In forests, plant growth happens in layers. The leafy tops of the trees reach high above the forest floor, where the leaves can get sunlight.

Woody shrubs catch the light that filters through the trees.

Ferns and mosses are scattered across the forest floor. Flowering plants often bloom in early spring, before the trees grow new leaves.

Temperate Deciduous Forest

- **Average Yearly Rainfall**
  75 to 125 cm (29.5 to 49 in.)
- **Average Temperatures**
  Summer: 28°C (82°F)
  Winter: 6°C (43°F)

Figure 2 *In a temperate deciduous forest, mammals, birds, and reptiles thrive on the many leaves, seeds, nuts, and insects.*

Forests

Forest biomes are often found in areas that have mild temperatures and plenty of rain. The kind of forest biome that develops depends on an area's temperatures and rainfall. Three forest biomes are temperate deciduous (dee SIJ oo uhs) forests, coniferous (koh NIF uhr uhs) forests, and tropical rain forests.

Temperate Deciduous Forests

Have you seen leaves change colors in the fall? Have you seen trees lose all of their leaves? If so, you have seen trees that are deciduous. The word *deciduous* comes from a Latin word that means "to fall off." Deciduous trees shed their leaves to save water during the winter or during the dry season. As shown in **Figure 2,** a variety of animals, such as bears, snakes, and woodpeckers, live in temperate deciduous forests.

Reading Check How does the word *deciduous* describe temperate deciduous forests? (*See the Appendix for answers to Reading Checks.*)

Coniferous Forest

- **Average Yearly Rainfall**
  35 to 75 cm (14 to 29.5 in.)
- **Average Temperatures**
  Summer: 14°C (57°F)
  Winter: −10°C (14°F)

These conifer leaves are adapted to conserve water.

A coniferous forest is home to many insects and to birds that eat those insects.

Herbivores that live in the coniferous forest include deer, moose, porcupines, and squirrels.

Figure 3 *Many animals that live in a coniferous forest survive the harsh winters by hibernating or migrating to a warmer climate for the winter.*

Coniferous Forests

Most of the trees in a coniferous forest are called *conifers*. Conifers produce seeds in cones. Conifers also have special leaves that are shaped like needles. The leaves have a thick, waxy coating. This waxy coating has three functions. First, it helps keep conifer leaves from drying out. Second, the waxy coating protects needles from being damaged by cold winter temperatures. Finally, the waxy coating allows most conifers to keep many of their leaves year-round. So, most conifers do not change very much from summer to winter. Trees that stay green all year and do not lose all of their leaves at one time are known as *evergreen trees*.

Figure 3 shows a coniferous forest and some of the animals that live there. Squirrels and insects live in coniferous forests. Birds, such as finches, chickadees, and jays, are common in these forests. Herbivores, such as porcupines, elk, and moose, also live in coniferous forests. The ground beneath large conifers is often covered by a thick layer of needles. Also, very little light reaches the ground. So, few large plants can grow beneath these trees.

Reading Check What is another name for most conifers? What are some animals that live in coniferous forests?

Tropical Rain Forests

Tropical rain forests have more biological diversity than other places on Earth have. This means that rain forests have more kinds of plants and animals than any other land biome. For example, more than 100 different kinds of trees may grow in an area about one-fourth the size of a football field. Many animals live on the ground. But most animals live in the *canopy,* or the treetops. Many different animals live in the canopy. For example, nearly 1,400 species of birds live in the rain-forest canopy. **Figure 4** shows some of the diversity of the tropical rain forest.

Because of its diversity, the rain forest may seem as if it has nutrient-rich soil. But most of the nutrients in the tropical rain forest are found in the plants. The soil is actually very thin and poor in nutrients. Because the soil is so thin, many trees grow above-ground roots for extra support.

Figure 4 *Tropical rain forests have a greater variety of organisms than any other biome.*

Trees form a continuous green roof, or canopy, that may extend 60 m above the forest floor.

Woody vines climb the tree trunks to reach sunlight.

Little light reaches the ground. Low-growing plants in the rain forest don't need a lot of light.

Tropical Rain Forest

- **Average Yearly Rainfall up to 400 cm (157.5 in.)**
- **Average Temperatures Daytime: 34°C (93°F) Nighttime: 20°C (68°F)**

Temperate Grassland

- Average Yearly Rainfall
  25 to 75 cm (10 to 29.5 in.)
- Average Temperatures
  Summer: 30°C (86°F)
  Winter: 0°C (32°F)

Figure 5 *Bison once roamed North American temperate grasslands in great herds.*

savanna a grassland that often has scattered trees and that is found in tropical and subtropical areas where seasonal rains, fires, and drought happen

CONNECTION TO Environmental Science

WRITING SKILL **Mountains and Climate**

Mountains can affect the climate of the land around them. Research the ecosystems around a mountain range. In your **science journal,** write a report describing how the mountains affect the climate of the surrounding land.

Grasslands

Grasslands have many names, such as *steppes, prairies,* and *pampas.* Grasslands are found on every continent but Antarctica. They are often flat or have gently rolling hills.

Temperate Grasslands

Temperate grassland plants include grasses and other flowering plants. Temperate grasslands have few trees. Fires, drought, and grazing prevent the growth of trees and shrubs. Temperate grasslands support small seed-eating animals, such as prairie dogs and mice. Large grass eaters, such as the North American bison shown in **Figure 5,** also live in temperate grasslands.

Savannas

A grassland that has scattered clumps of trees and seasonal rains is called a **savanna.** Savannas are found in parts of Africa, India, and South America. During the dry season, savanna grasses dry out and turn yellow. But the grasses' deep roots survive for many months without water. The African savanna is home to many large herbivores, such as elephants, giraffes, zebras, and wildebeests. Some of these animals are shown in **Figure 6.**

Reading Check What happens to grasses on a savanna during the dry season?

Savanna

- Average Yearly Rainfall
  150 cm (59 in.)
- Average Temperatures
  Dry season: 34°C (93°F)
  Wet season: 16°C (61°F)

Figure 6 *In the African savanna, lions and leopards hunt zebras and wildebeests.*

Cactuses store water in their stems and roots.

Some flowering plants bloom, bear seeds, and die within a few weeks after a heavy rain.

Deep-rooted plants can reach groundwater as deep as 30 m.

Huge ears help jack rabbits get rid of body heat.

Kangaroo rats never need to drink. They recycle water from the foods that they eat.

Figure 7 *The residents of the desert biome have special adaptations to survive in a dry climate.*

Deserts

Biomes that are very dry and often very hot are called **deserts.** Many kinds of plants and animals are found only in deserts. These organisms have special adaptations to live in a hot, dry climate. For example, plants grow far apart so that the plants won't have to compete with each other for water. Some plants have shallow, widespread roots that grow just under the surface. These roots let plants take up water during a storm. Other desert plants, such as cactuses, have fleshy stems and leaves. These fleshy structures store water. The leaves of desert plants also have a waxy coating that helps prevent water loss.

Animals also have adaptations for living in the desert. Most desert animals are active only at night, when temperatures are cooler. Some animals, such as the spadefoot toad, bury themselves in the ground and are dormant during the dry season. Doing so helps these animals escape the heat of summer. Animals such as desert tortoises eat flowers or leaves and store the water under their shells. **Figure 7** shows how some desert plants and animals live in the heat with little water.

desert a region that has little or no plant life, long periods without rain, and extreme temperatures; usually found in hot climates

✓ **Reading Check** What are some adaptations of desert plants?

Tundra

- **Average Yearly Rainfall**
  30 to 50 cm (12 to 20 in.)
- **Average Temperatures**
  Summer: 12°C (54°F)
  Winter: −26°C (−15°F)

Figure 8 *During winters in the tundra, caribou migrate to grazing grounds that have a more-plentiful supply of food.*

tundra a treeless plain found in the Arctic, in the Antarctic, or on the tops of mountains that is characterized by very low winter temperatures and short, cool summers

Local Ecosystems

WRITING SKILL With a family member, explore the ecosystems around your home. What kinds of plants and animals live in your area? In your **science journal,** write a short essay describing the plants and animals in the ecosystems near your home.

Tundra

Imagine a place on Earth where it is so cold that trees do not grow. A biome that has very cold temperatures and little rainfall is called a **tundra.** Two types of tundra are polar tundra and alpine tundra.

Polar Tundra

Polar tundra is found near the North and South Poles. In polar tundra, the layer of soil beneath the surface soil stays frozen all the time. This layer is called *permafrost.* During the short, cool summers, only the surface soil thaws. The layer of thawed soil is too shallow for deep-rooted plants to live. So, shallow-rooted plants, such as grasses and small shrubs, are common. Mosses and lichens (LIE kuhnz) grow beneath these plants. The thawed soil above the permafrost becomes muddy. Insects, such as mosquitoes, lay eggs in the mud. Birds feed on these insects. Other tundra animals include musk oxen, wolves, and caribou, such as the one shown in **Figure 8.**

Alpine Tundra

Alpine tundra is similar to arctic tundra. Alpine tundra also has permafrost. But alpine tundra is found at the top of tall mountains. Above an elevation called the *tree line*, trees cannot grow on a mountain. Alpine tundra is found above the tree line. Alpine tundra gets plenty of sunlight and precipitation.

✓ Reading Check What is alpine tundra?

Summary

- A biome is characterized by abiotic factors, such as climate, and biotic factors, such as plant and animal communities.

- Three forest biomes are temperate deciduous forests, coniferous forests, and tropical rain forests.

- Grasslands are areas where grasses are the main plants. Temperate grasslands have hot summers and cold winters. Savannas have wet and dry seasons.

- Deserts are very dry and often very hot. Desert plants and animals competing for the limited water supply have special adaptations for survival.

- Tundras are cold areas that have very little rainfall. Permafrost, the layer of frozen soil below the surface of arctic tundra, determines the kinds of plants and animals that live on the tundra.

Using Key Terms

1. Use each of the following terms in a separate sentence: *biome* and *tundra*.

2. In your own words, write a definition for each of the following terms: *savanna* and *desert*.

Understanding Key Ideas

3. If you visited a savanna, you would most likely see
   a. large herds of grazing animals, such as zebras, gazelles, and wildebeests.
   b. dense forests stretching from horizon to horizon.
   c. snow and ice throughout most of the year.
   d. trees that form a continuous green roof, called the *canopy*.

4. Components of a desert ecosystem include
   a. a hot, dry climate.
   b. plants that grow far apart.
   c. animals that are active mostly at night.
   d. All of the above

5. List seven land biomes that are found on Earth.

6. What are two things that characterize a biome?

Critical Thinking

7. **Making Inferences** While excavating an area in the desert, a scientist discovers the fossils of very large trees and ferns. What might the scientist conclude about biomes in this area?

8. **Analyzing Ideas** Tundra receives very little rainfall. Could tundra accurately be called a *frozen desert*? Explain your answer.

Interpreting Graphics

Use the bar graph below to answer the questions that follow.

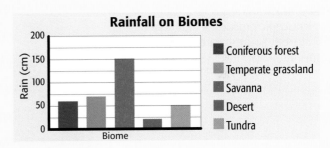

Rainfall on Biomes

Rain (cm) — 200, 150, 100, 50, 0
Biome

- Coniferous forest
- Temperate grassland
- Savanna
- Desert
- Tundra

9. Which biomes receive 50 cm or more of rain each year?

10. Which biome receives the smallest amount of rain? the largest amount of rain?

SCLINKS

NSTA
Developed and maintained by the
National Science Teachers Association

For a variety of links related to this chapter, go to www.scilinks.org

Topic: Forests
SciLinks code: HSM0609

Marine Ecosystems

What covers almost three-fourths of Earth's surface? What holds both the largest animals and some of the smallest organisms on Earth?

If your answer to both questions is *oceans,* you are correct! Earth's oceans contain many different ecosystems. Scientists call ecosystems in the ocean *marine ecosystems.*

Life in the Ocean

Marine ecosystems are shaped by abiotic factors. These factors include water temperature, water depth, and the amount of sunlight that passes into the water. The animals and plants that live in the ocean come in all shapes and sizes. The largest animals on Earth, blue whales, live in the ocean. So do trillions of tiny plankton. **Plankton** are tiny organisms that float near the surface of the water. Many plankton are producers. They use photosynthesis to make their own food. Plankton form the base of the ocean's food chains. **Figure 1** shows plankton and an animal that relies on plankton for food.

Reading Check What are plankton? How are they important to marine ecosystems? (*See the Appendix for answers to Reading Checks.*)

What You Will Learn

- List three abiotic factors that shape marine ecosystems.
- Describe four major ocean zones.
- Describe five marine ecosystems.

Vocabulary

plankton
estuary

READING STRATEGY

Prediction Guide Before reading this section, write the title of each heading in this section. Next, under each heading, write what you think you will learn.

plankton the mass of mostly microscopic organisms that float or drift freely in freshwater and marine environments

Figure 1 *Marine ecosystems support a broad diversity of life. Humpback whales rely on plankton for food.*

Temperature

The temperature of ocean water decreases as the depth of the water increases. However, the temperature change is not gradual. **Figure 2** shows the three temperature zones of ocean water. Notice that the temperature of the water in the surface zone is much warmer than in the rest of the ocean. Temperatures in the surface zone vary with latitude. Areas of the ocean along the equator are warmer than areas closer to the poles. Surface zone temperatures also vary with the time of year. During the summer, the Northern Hemisphere is tilted toward the sun. So, the surface zone is warmer than it is during the winter.

Temperature affects the animals that live in marine ecosystems. For example, fishes that live near the poles have adaptations to live in near-freezing water. In contrast, animals that live in coral reefs need warm water to live. Some animals, such as whales, migrate from cold areas to warm areas of the ocean to reproduce. Water temperature also affects whether some animals, such as barnacles, can eat. If the water is too hot or too cold, these animals may not be able to eat. A sudden change in temperature may cause these animals to die.

✓ Reading Check How does temperature affect marine animals?

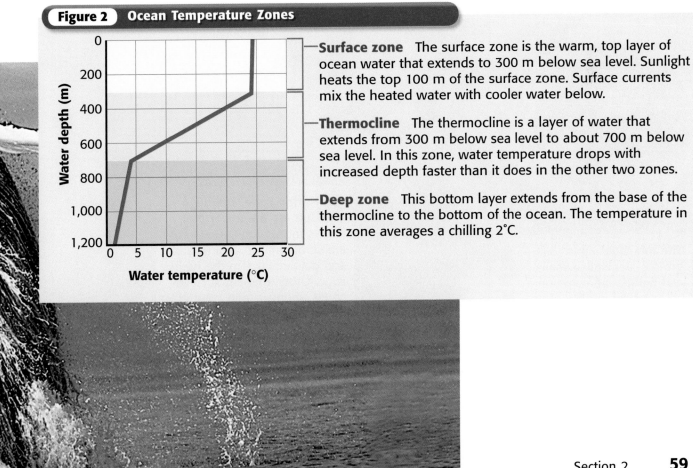

Figure 2 **Ocean Temperature Zones**

Water depth (m) / Water temperature (°C)

—**Surface zone** The surface zone is the warm, top layer of ocean water that extends to 300 m below sea level. Sunlight heats the top 100 m of the surface zone. Surface currents mix the heated water with cooler water below.

—**Thermocline** The thermocline is a layer of water that extends from 300 m below sea level to about 700 m below sea level. In this zone, water temperature drops with increased depth faster than it does in the other two zones.

—**Deep zone** This bottom layer extends from the base of the thermocline to the bottom of the ocean. The temperature in this zone averages a chilling 2°C.

Depth and Sunlight

In addition to water temperature, life in the ocean is affected by water depth and the amount of sunlight that passes into the water. The major ocean zones are shown in **Figure 3.**

The Intertidal Zone

The intertidal zone is the place where the ocean meets the land. This area is exposed to the air for part of the day. Waves are always crashing on the rock and sand. The animals that live in the intertidal zone have adaptations to survive exposure to air and to keep from being washed away by the waves.

The Neritic Zone

As you move farther away from shore, into the neritic zone (nee RIT ik ZOHN), the water becomes deeper. The ocean floor starts to slope downward. The water is warm and receives a lot of sunlight. Many interesting plants and animals, such as corals, sea turtles, fishes, and dolphins, live in this zone.

Figure 3 *The life in a marine ecosystem depends on water temperature, water depth, and the amount of sunlight the area receives.*

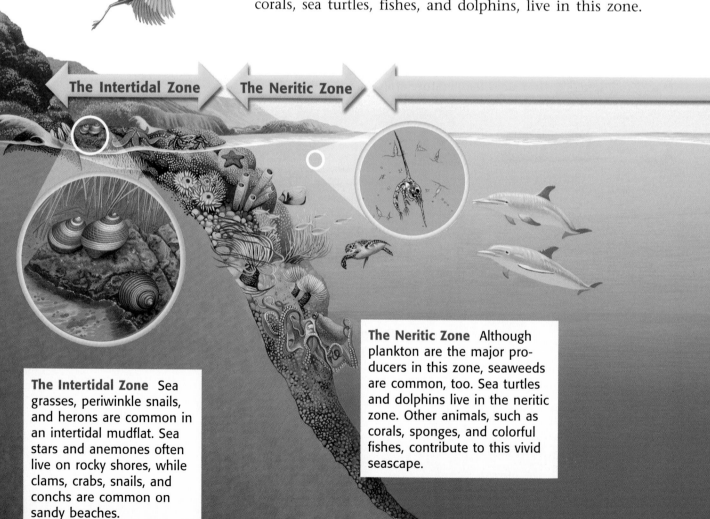

The Intertidal Zone Sea grasses, periwinkle snails, and herons are common in an intertidal mudflat. Sea stars and anemones often live on rocky shores, while clams, crabs, snails, and conchs are common on sandy beaches.

The Neritic Zone Although plankton are the major producers in this zone, seaweeds are common, too. Sea turtles and dolphins live in the neritic zone. Other animals, such as corals, sponges, and colorful fishes, contribute to this vivid seascape.

The Intertidal Zone

The Neritic Zone

The Oceanic Zone

In the oceanic zone, the sea floor drops sharply. This zone contains the deep water of the open ocean. Plankton can be found near the water surface. Animals, such as fishes, whales, and sharks, are found in the oceanic zone. Some animals in this zone live in very deep water. These animals often get food from material that sinks down from the ocean surface.

The Benthic Zone

The benthic zone is the ocean floor. The deepest parts of the benthic zone do not get any sunlight. They are also very cold. Animals, such as fishes, worms, and crabs, have special adaptations to the deep, dark water. Many of these organisms get food by eating material that sinks from above. Some organisms, such as bacteria, get energy from chemicals that escape from thermal vents on the ocean floor. Thermal vents form at cracks in the Earth's crust.

✔ Reading Check How do animals in the benthic zone get food?

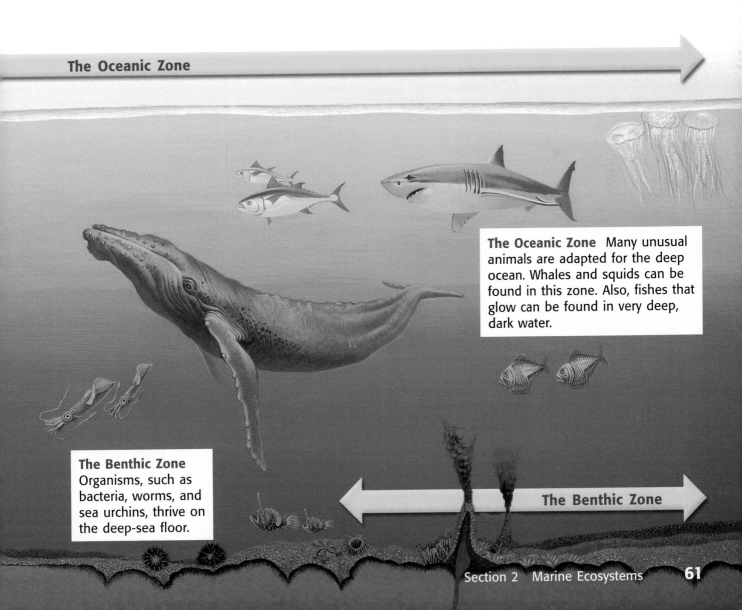

The Oceanic Zone

The Oceanic Zone Many unusual animals are adapted for the deep ocean. Whales and squids can be found in this zone. Also, fishes that glow can be found in very deep, dark water.

The Benthic Zone Organisms, such as bacteria, worms, and sea urchins, thrive on the deep-sea floor.

The Benthic Zone

A Closer Look

Life on Earth depends on the ocean. Through evaporation, the ocean provides most of the water that makes up Earth's precipitation. Ocean temperatures and currents can affect world climates and wind patterns. Humans and many animals depend on the ocean for food.

Many ecosystems exist in the ocean. Some of these ecosystems are found on or near the shore. Other ecosystems are found in the middle of the ocean or near the poles.

Intertidal Areas

estuary an area where fresh water from rivers mixes with salt water from the ocean

Intertidal areas are found near the shore. These areas include mudflats, sandy beaches, and rocky shores. Intertidal organisms must be able to live both underwater and out of water. The organisms that live in mudflats include worms and crabs. Shorebirds feed on these animals. Organisms that live on sandy beaches include worms, clams, crabs, and plankton. On rocky shores, organisms have adaptations to keep from being swept away by crashing waves. Some organisms use rootlike structures called *holdfasts* to attach themselves to the rocks. Other organisms attach themselves to rocks by releasing a special glue.

Coral Reefs

Most coral reefs are found in warm, shallow areas of the neritic zone. The reefs are made up of small animals called *corals*. Corals live in large groups. When corals die, they leave their skeletons behind. New corals grow on these remains. Over time, layers of skeletons build up and form a reef. This reef provides a home for many marine animals and plants. These organisms include algae, brightly colored fishes, sponges, sea stars, and sea urchins. An example of a coral reef is shown in **Figure 4.**

✓ Reading Check How do coral reefs develop?

Estuaries

An area where fresh water from streams and rivers spills into the ocean is called an **estuary** (ES tyoo er ee). In estuaries, the fresh water from rivers and the salt water from the ocean are always mixing. Therefore, the amount of salt in the water is always changing. Plants and animals that live in estuaries must be able to survive the changing concentrations of salt. The fresh water that spills into an estuary is rich in nutrients. Because estuaries are so nutrient rich, they support large numbers of plankton. The plankton, in turn, provide food for many animals.

Figure 4 *A coral reef is one of the most biologically diverse ecosystems on Earth.*

The Sargasso Sea

An ecosystem called the *Sargasso Sea* (sahr GAS oh SEE) is found in the middle of the Atlantic Ocean. This ecosystem contains floating rafts of algae called *sargassums* (sahr GAS uhmz). Many of the animals that live in the Sargasso Sea are the same color as sargassums, which helps the animals hide from predators.

Polar Ice

The Arctic Ocean and the ocean around Antarctica make up another marine ecosystem. These icy waters are rich in nutrients, which support large numbers of plankton. Many fishes, birds, and mammals rely on the plankton for food. Animals, such as polar bears and penguins, live on the polar ice.

SECTION Review

Summary

- Abiotic factors that affect marine ecosystems are water temperature, water depth, and the amount of light that passes into the water.
- Plankton form the base of the ocean's food chains.
- Four ocean zones are the intertidal zone, the neritic zone, the oceanic zone, and the benthic zone.
- The ocean contains unique ecosystems, including intertidal areas, coral reefs, estuaries, the Sargasso Sea, and polar ice.

Using Key Terms

1. Use each of the following terms in a separate sentence: *plankton* and *estuary*.

Understanding Key Ideas

2. Water temperature
   a. has no effect on the animals in a marine ecosystem.
   b. affects the types of organisms that can live in a marine ecosystem.
   c. decreases gradually as water gets deeper.
   d. increases as water gets deeper.

3. What are three abiotic factors that affect marine ecosystems?

4. Describe four major ocean zones.

5. Describe five marine ecosystems. For each ecosystem, list an organism that lives there.

Math Skills

6. The ocean covers about 71% of the Earth's surface. If the total surface area of the Earth is about 510 million square kilometers, how many square kilometers are covered by the ocean?

Critical Thinking

7. **Making Inferences** Animals in the Sargasso Sea hide from predators by blending in with the sargassum. Color is only one way to blend in. What is another way that animals can blend in with sargassum?

8. **Identifying Relationships** Many fishes and other organisms that live in the deep ocean produce light. What are two ways in which this light might be useful?

9. **Applying Concepts** Imagine that you are studying animals that live in intertidal zones. You just discovered a new animal. Describe the animal and adaptations the animal has to survive in the intertidal zone.

Freshwater Ecosystems

A brook bubbles over rocks. A mighty river thunders through a canyon. A calm swamp echoes with the sounds of frogs and birds. What do these places have in common?

Brooks, rivers, and swamps are examples of freshwater eco-systems. The water in brooks and rivers is often fast moving. In swamps, water moves very slowly. Also, water in swamps is often found in standing pools.

Stream and River Ecosystems

The water in brooks, streams, and rivers may flow from melting ice or snow. Or the water may come from a spring. A spring is a place where water flows from underground to the Earth's surface. Each stream of water that joins a larger stream is called a *tributary* (TRIB yoo TER ee). As more tributaries join a stream, the stream contains more water. The stream becomes stronger and wider. A very strong, wide stream is called a *river*. **Figure 1** shows how a river develops.

Like other ecosystems, freshwater ecosystems are character-ized by their abiotic factors. An important abiotic factor in freshwater ecosystems is how quickly water moves.

Streams and rivers are full of life. Plants line the edges of streams and rivers. Fish live in the open waters. And clams and snails live in the mud at the bottom of a stream or river. Organisms that live in fast-moving water have adaptations to keep from being washed away. Some producers, such as algae and moss, are attached to rocks. Consumers, such as tadpoles, use suction disks to hold themselves to rocks. Other consum-ers, such as insects, live under rocks.

What You Will Learn

- Describe one abiotic factor that affects freshwater ecosystems.
- Describe the three zones of a lake.
- Describe two wetland ecosystems.
- Explain how a lake becomes a forest.

Vocabulary

littoral zone   wetland
open-water zone   marsh
deep-water zone   swamp

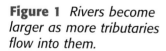
READING STRATEGY

Paired Summarizing Read this section silently. In pairs, take turns summarizing the material. Stop to discuss ideas that seem confusing.

Figure 1 *Rivers become larger as more tributaries flow into them.*

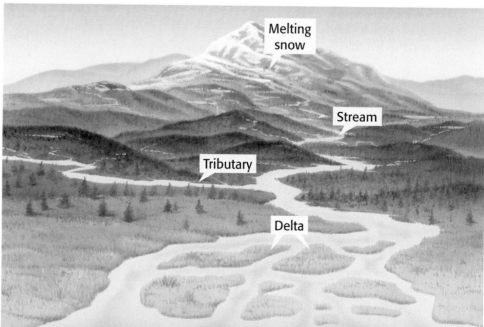

Melting snow

Stream

Tributary

Delta

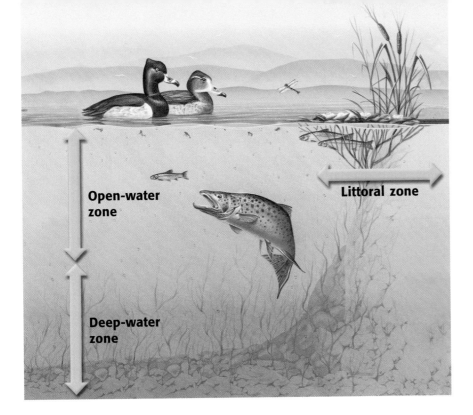

Open-water zone

Littoral zone

Deep-water zone

Figure 2 *Ponds and lakes can be divided into three zones. Each zone has different organisms and abiotic factors.*

Pond and Lake Ecosystems

Ponds and lakes have different ecosystems than streams and rivers do. **Figure 2** shows the zones of a typical lake.

Life near Shore

The area of water closest to the edge of a lake or pond is called the **littoral zone** (LIT uh ruhl ZOHN). Sunlight reaches the bottom of the littoral zone. This sunlight makes it possible for algae and plants to grow in the littoral zone. Algae grow beneath the surface of the water in the littoral zone. Plants that grow near the shore include cattails and rushes. Floating leaf plants, such as water lilies, grow farther from the shore. The plants of the littoral zone are home to small animals, such as snails and insects. Clams and worms bury themselves in the mud. Frogs, salamanders, turtles, fish, and snakes also live in this zone.

Life Away from Shore

The area of a lake or pond that extends from the littoral zone across the top of the water is called the **open-water zone.** The open-water zone goes as deep as sunlight can reach. This zone is home to bass, lake trout, and other fishes. Many photosynthetic plankton also live in this area. Beneath the open-water zone is the **deep-water zone,** where no sunlight reaches. Catfish, carp, worms, crustaceans, fungi, and bacteria live here. These organisms often feed on dead organisms that sink from above.

✓ Reading Check Describe the three zones of a lake. (*See the Appendix for answers to Reading Checks.*)

Pond-Food Relationships

1. On **index cards,** write the names of some of the plants and animals that live in a typical freshwater pond or small lake. Write one type of organism on each card.

2. Use **yarn** or **string** to connect each organism to its food sources.

3. Describe the food relationships in a pond.

littoral zone the shallow zone of a lake or pond where light reaches the bottom and nurtures plants

open-water zone the zone of a pond or lake that extends from the littoral zone and that is only as deep as light can reach

deep-water zone the zone of a lake or pond below the open-water zone, where no light reaches

Figure 3 *This painted turtle suns itself on a log in a freshwater marsh.*

Wetland Ecosystems

An area of land that is sometimes underwater or whose soil contains a great deal of moisture is called a **wetland.** Wetlands support many different plants and animals. Wetlands also play an important role in flood control. During heavy rains or spring snow melt, wetlands soak up large amounts of water. The water in wetlands also moves deeper into the ground. So, wetlands help replenish underground water supplies.

Marshes

A treeless wetland ecosystem where plants, such as grasses, grow is called a **marsh.** A freshwater marsh is shown in **Figure 3.** Freshwater marshes are often found in shallow areas along the shores of lakes, ponds, rivers, and streams. The plants in a marsh vary depending on the depth of the water and the location of the marsh. Grasses, reeds, bulrushes, and wild rice are common marsh plants. Muskrats, turtles, frogs, and birds also live in marshes.

Swamps

A wetland ecosystem in which trees and vines grow is called a **swamp.** Swamps, as shown in **Figure 4,** are found in low-lying areas and beside slow-moving rivers. Most swamps are flooded part of the year, depending on rainfall. Willows, bald cypresses, and oaks are common swamp trees. Vines, such as poison ivy, grow up tree trunks. Plants, such as orchids, may hang from tree branches. Water lilies and other plants grow in standing water. Many fishes, snakes, and birds also live in swamps.

Reading Check What is a swamp?

CONNECTION TO Language Arts

Compound Words A compound word is a word made up of two or more single words. In your **science journal,** define the two words that make up the word *wetland.* Then, define three more compound words.

Figure 4 *The trunks of these trees are adapted to give the trees more support in the wet, soft soil of a swamp.*

From a Lake to a Forest

Did you know that a lake or pond can disappear? How can this happen? Water entering a standing body of water usually carries nutrients and sediment. These materials settle to the bottom of the pond or lake. Dead leaves from overhanging trees and decaying plant and animal life also settle to the bottom. Then, bacteria decompose this material. This process uses oxygen in the water. The loss of oxygen affects the kinds of animals that can survive in the pond or lake. For example, many fishes would not be able to survive with less oxygen in the water.

Over time, the pond or lake is filled with sediment. Plants grow in the new soil. Shallow areas fill in first. So, plants slowly grow closer and closer to the center of the pond or lake. What is left of the lake or pond becomes a wetland, such as a marsh or swamp. Eventually, the wetland can become a forest.

✓ Reading Check What happens to some of the animals in a pond as the pond becomes a forest?

INTERNET ACTIVITY

For another activity related to this chapter, go to **go.hrw.com** and type in the keyword **HL5ECOW**.

SECTION Review

Summary

- An important abiotic factor in freshwater ecosystems is how quickly water moves.
- The three zones of a pond or lake are the littoral zone, the open-water zone, and the deep-water zone.
- Wetlands include marshes and swamps.
- Sediments and decaying plant and animal matter build up in a pond. Over time, the pond may fill completely and become a forest.

Using Key Terms

1. Use the following terms in the same sentence: *wetland, marsh,* and *swamp.*

Understanding Key Ideas

2. A major abiotic factor in freshwater ecosystems is the
   a. source of the water.
   b. speed of the water.
   c. width of the stream or river.
   d. None of the above

3. Describe the three zones of a lake.

4. Explain how a lake can become a forest over time.

Math Skills

5. Sunlight can penetrate a certain lake to a depth of 15 m. The lake is five and a half times deeper than the depth to which light can penetrate. In meters, how deep is the lake?

Critical Thinking

6. **Making Inferences** When bacteria decompose material in a pond, the oxygen in the water may be used up. So, fishes in the pond die. How might the absence of fish lead to a pond filling faster?

7. **Applying Concepts** Imagine a steep, rocky stream. What kinds of adaptations might animals living in this stream have? Explain your answer.

SCiLINKS

NSTA
Developed and maintained by the National Science Teachers Association

For a variety of links related to this chapter, go to www.scilinks.org

Topic: Freshwater Ecosystems
SciLinks code: HSM0621

Skills Practice Lab

OBJECTIVES

Draw common pond-water organisms.

Observe the effect of fertilizer on pond-water organisms.

Describe how fertilizer affects the number and type of pond-water organisms over time.

MATERIALS

- beaker, 500 mL
- distilled water, 2.25 L
- eyedropper
- fertilizer
- gloves, protective
- graduated cylinder, 100 mL
- jars, 1 qt or 1 L (3)
- microscope
- microscope slides with coverslips
- pencil, wax
- plastic wrap
- pond water containing living organisms, 300 mL
- stirring rod

SAFETY

Too Much of a Good Thing?

Plants need nutrients, such as phosphates and nitrates, to grow. Phosphates are often found in detergents. Nitrates are often found in animal wastes and fertilizers. When large amounts of these nutrients enter rivers and lakes, algae and plants grow rapidly and then die off. Microorganisms that decompose the dead matter use up oxygen in the water. Without oxygen, fish and other animals die. In this activity, you will observe the effect of fertilizers on organisms that live in pond water.

Procedure

1. Label one jar "Control," the second jar "Fertilizer," and the third jar "Excess fertilizer."

2. Pour 750 mL of distilled water into each jar. To the "Fertilizer" jar, add the amount of fertilizer recommended for 750 mL of water. To the "Excess fertilizer" jar, add 10 times the amount recommended for 750 mL of water. Stir the contents of each jar to dissolve the fertilizer.

3. Obtain a sample of pond water. Stir it gently to make sure that the organisms in it are evenly distributed. Pour 100 mL of pond water into each of the three jars.

4. Observe a drop of water from each jar under the microscope. Draw at least four of the organisms. Determine whether the organisms you see are producers, which are usually green, or consumers, which are usually able to move. Describe the number and type of organisms in the pond water.

Common Pond-Water Organisms

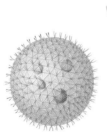   

Volvox
(producer)

Spirogyra
(producer)

Daphnia
(consumer)

Vorticella
(consumer)

5. Cover each jar loosely with plastic wrap. Place the jars near a sunny window but not in direct sunlight.

6. Make a prediction about how the pond organisms will grow in each of the three jars.

7. Make three data tables. Title one table "Control," as shown below. Title another table "Fertilizer," and title the third table "Excess fertilizer."

Control			
Date	Color	Odor	Other observations
	DO NOT WRITE IN BOOK		

8. Observe the jars when you first set them up and once every 3 days for the next 3 weeks. Note the color, the odor, and the presence of organisms. Record your observations.

9. When organisms become visible in the jars, use an eyedropper to remove a sample from each jar. Observe the sample under the microscope. How have the number and type of organisms changed since you first looked at the pond water?

10. At the end of the 3-week period, observe a sample from each jar under the microscope. Draw at least four of the most abundant organisms, and describe how the number and type of organisms have changed since your last microscope observation.

Analyze the Results

1. **Describing Events** After 3 weeks, which jar has the most abundant growth of algae?

2. **Analyzing Data** Did you observe any effects on organisms (other than algae) in the jar with the most abundant algal growth? Explain your answer.

Draw Conclusions

3. **Drawing Conclusions** What may have caused increased growth in the jars?

4. **Evaluating Results** Did your observations match your predictions? Explain your answer.

5. **Interpreting Information** Decaying plant and animal life contribute to the filling of lakes and ponds. How might the rapid filling of lakes and ponds be prevented or slowed?

Chapter Review

USING KEY TERMS

1 In your own words, write a definition for the following terms: *biome* and *tundra*.

2 Use each of the following terms in a separate sentence: *intertidal zone, neritic zone,* and *oceanic zone.*

For each pair of terms, explain how the meanings of the terms differ.

3 *savanna* and *desert*

4 *open-water zone* and *deep-water zone*

5 *marsh* and *swamp*

UNDERSTANDING KEY IDEAS

Multiple Choice

6 Trees that lose their leaves in the winter are called

  a. evergreen trees.

  b. coniferous trees.

  c. deciduous trees.

  d. None of the above

7 In which major ocean zone are plants and animals exposed to air for part of the day?

  a. intertidal zone

  b. neritic zone

  c. oceanic zone

  d. benthic zone

8 An abiotic factor that affects marine ecosystems is

  a. the temperature of the water.

  b. the depth of the water.

  c. the amount of sunlight that passes through the water.

  d. All of the above

9 _____ is a marine ecosystem that includes mudflats, sandy beaches, and rocky shores.

  a. An intertidal area

  b. Polar ice

  c. A coral reef

  d. The Sargasso Sea

Short Answer

10 What are seven land biomes?

11 Explain how a small lake can become a forest.

12 What are two factors that characterize biomes?

13 Describe the three zones of a lake.

14 How do rivers form?

15 What are three abiotic factors in land biomes? three abiotic factors in marine ecosystems? an abiotic factor in fresh-water ecosystems?

16 Concept Mapping Use the following terms to create a concept map: *plants and animals, tropical rain forest, tundra, biomes, permafrost, canopy, desert,* and *abiotic factors.*

17 Making Inferences Plankton use photosynthesis to make their own food. They need sunlight for photosynthesis. Which of the four major ocean zones can support plankton growth? Explain your answer.

18 Predicting Consequences Wetlands, such as marshes and swamps, play an important role in flood control. Wetlands also help replenish underground water supplies. Predict what might happen if a wetland dries out.

19 Analyzing Ideas A scientist has a new hypothesis. He or she thinks that savannas and deserts are part of one biome rather than two separate biomes. Based on what you've learned, decide if the scientist's hypothesis is correct. Explain your answer.

20 Applying Concepts Imagine that you are a scientist. You are studying an area that gets about 100 cm of rain each year. The average summer temperatures are near 30°C. What biome are you in? What are some plants and animals you will likely encounter? If you stayed in this area for the winter, what kind of preparations might you need to make?

Use the graphs below to answer the questions that follow.

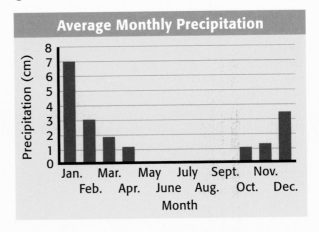

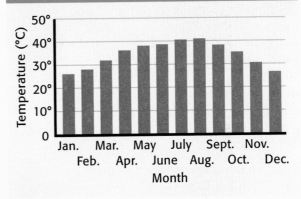

21 Which biome is most likely found in the region described by the graphs above? Explain your answer.

22 How many centimeters of rain fell in the region during the course of the year?

23 Which month is the hottest in the region? the coolest in the region?

24 What is the average monthly precipitation for the month that has the highest average high temperature?

Standardized Test Preparation

Read each of the passages below. Then, answer the questions that follow each passage.

Passage 1 Billy has a brochure for a camp that boasts of being the most adventurous summer camp in the world. Billy can't wait to go to the camp and have fun outdoors. To prepare, he checks the supply list, which includes the following: light, summer clothes; sunscreen; rain gear; a heavy, down-filled jacket; a ski mask; and thick gloves. The list seems strange to Billy. He thought he was traveling to only one <u>destination</u>, so why does he need to bring such a wide variety of clothes? Billy rereads the brochure and learns that the campers will "climb the biomes of the world in just three days." The destination is Africa's tallest mountain, Kilimanjaro.

1. In this passage, what does the word *destination* likely mean?
   A camp
   B vacation
   C place
   D mountain

2. Based on the passage, which of the following statements is a fact?
   F People ski on Kilimanjaro.
   G Kilimanjaro is Africa's tallest mountain.
   H It rains a lot on Kilimanjaro.
   I The summers are cold on Kilimanjaro.

3. Why might Billy wonder if the brochure was advertising only one location?
   A The brochure called the camp the most adventurous summer camp in the world.
   B The brochure said that he would need light, summer clothes and sunscreen.
   C The brochure said that he would need light, summer clothes and a heavy, down-filled jacket.
   D The brochure said that the summers are cold on Kilimanjaro.

Passage 2 The layer of soil above the permafrost is too shallow for plants with deep roots to live. Grasses and shrubs can survive there because they have shallow roots. A sheet of mosses and lichens grows beneath these plants. When the soil above the permafrost thaws, the soil becomes muddy. Muddy soil is an excellent place for insects, such as mosquitoes, to lay eggs. Many birds spend the summer in the tundra to feed on these insects. Tundra animals include caribou, musk oxen, wolves, and other large mammals. Smaller animals, such as lemmings, shrews, and hares, also live in the tundra.

1. Based on the passage, what is one reason for the lack of trees on the tundra?
   A Trees need more sunlight than is available.
   B The roots of trees need more room than is available.
   C The soil above the permafrost becomes too muddy for trees.
   D Trees need more water than is available.

2. Based on the passage, which of the following statements about permafrost is true?
   F It is a thawed layer of soil.
   G It is always moist.
   H It is always frozen.
   I It is shallow.

3. Based on the passage, which of the following statements is a fact?
   A Muddy soil is an excellent place for mosses and lichens to grow.
   B Birds fly north to reach the tundra in the summer.
   C Caribou and oxen are some of the large mammals that live in the tundra.
   D The tundra is a beautiful biome that is home to diverse communities.

The map below shows the biomes of Australia. Use the map to answer the questions that follow.

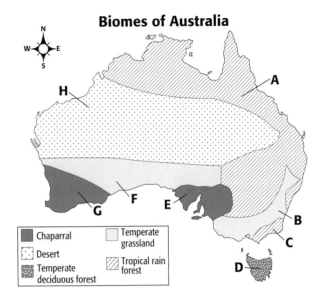

Biomes of Australia

Legend:
- Chaparral
- Desert
- Temperate deciduous forest
- Temperate grassland
- Tropical rain forest

1. Which letters on the map correspond to areas that are chaparral?
   A A and C
   B B and F
   C C and E
   D E and G

2. If you lived in the area marked F, which biome would you live in?
   F desert
   G temperate grassland
   H temperate deciduous forest
   I tropical rain forest

3. If you wanted to live in a forest, which letters correspond to areas where you could live?
   A A, B, and D
   B A, C, and D
   C B, C, and D
   D C, D, and E

4. Which letter corresponds to desert?
   F A
   G D
   H F
   I H

Read each question below, and choose the best answer.

1. Larry wants to buy a glass tabletop for his science lab at home. The glass tabletop is 1 m wide and 2 m long. How many square meters is the surface of the glass tabletop?
   A 2 m
   B 2 m^2
   C 3 m^2
   D 6 m^2

2. A scuba diver was exploring a coral reef. She spent 1.5 h exploring on Friday and spent twice as many hours exploring on Saturday. Which equation could be used to find n, the total number of hours that the scuba diver spent exploring on Friday and Saturday?
   F $n = 2 \div 1.5$
   G $n = 1.5 + (2 \times 1.5)$
   H $n = 1.5 + 1.5 + 2$
   I $n = 2 \times 1.5$

3. How do you express $5 \times 5 \times 5 \times 5 \times 2 \times 2 \times 2$ in exponential notation?
   A $(5 \times 4) + (2 \times 3)$
   B $5^4 \times 2^3$
   C $4^5 \times 3^2$
   D $5^7 \times 2^7$

4. The tropical rain forest receives up to 400 cm of rain per year. The desert receives up to 25 cm of rain per year. Which of the following simplified fractions compares rainfall in the desert to rainfall in the rain forest?
   F 1/400
   G 1/25
   H 1/16
   I 16

Standardized Test Preparation   73

Science in Action

Scientific Debate

Developing Wetlands

Wetlands are home to many flowering plants, birds, and turtles. Wetlands also play important roles in flood control and maintaining water quality. However, as more people need homes, grocery stores, and other facilities, some wetlands are being developed for construction. State governments often regulate the development of wetlands. Development is not allowed on many environmentally sensitive wetlands. But it is sometimes allowed on wetlands that are less sensitive. However, some people think that all wetlands should be protected, regardless of how sensitive an area is.

Scientific Discoveries

Ocean Vents

Imagine the deepest parts of the ocean. There is no light at all, and it is very cold. Some of the animals that live here have found a unique place to live—vents on the ocean floor. Water seeps into the Earth between plates on the ocean floor. The water is heated and absorbs sulfuric gases. When the water blasts up through ocean vents, it raises the temperature of the ocean hundreds of degrees! Bacteria use the gases from the ocean vents to survive. In turn, mussels and clams feed on the bacteria. Without ocean vents, it would be much more difficult for these organisms to survive.

Language Arts ACTIVITY

WRITING SKILL Research wetland development on your own. Then, write a letter in which you describe your opinion about the development of wetlands.

Math ACTIVITY

A thermal vent increases the temperature of the water around it to 360°C. If the temperature of the water was 2°C, what is the difference in temperature? By what percentage did the water temperature increase?

Alfonso Alonso-Mejía

Ecologist During the winter, ecologist Alfonso Alonso-Mejía visits sites in central Mexico where millions of monarch butterflies spend the winter. Unfortunately, the monarchs' winter habitat is threatened by human activity. Only nine of the monarchs' wintering sites remain. Five of the sites are set aside as sanctuaries for monarchs, but these sites are threatened by people who cut down fir trees for firewood or for commercial purposes.

Alonso-Mejía discovered that monarchs depend on understory vegetation, bushlike plants that grow beneath fir trees, to survive. When the temperature is low, monarchs can climb understory vegetation until they are at least 10 cm above the ground. This tiny difference in elevation can ensure that monarchs are warm enough to survive. Because of Alonso-Mejía's discovery, Mexican conservationists are working to protect understory vegetation and monarchs.

Social Studies ACTiViTy

Use your school library or the Internet to research the routes that monarchs use to migrate to Mexico. Draw a map illustrating your findings.

To learn more about these Science in Action topics, visit **go.hrw.com** and type in the keyword **HL5ECOF**.

Current Science

Check out Current Science® articles related to this chapter by visiting **go.hrw.com**. Just type in the keyword **HL5CS20**.

4

Environmental Problems and Solutions

The Big Idea

Human activities affect the environment in positive and negative ways.

SECTION

1 **Environmental Problems**...... 78

2 **Environmental Solutions**...... 84

About the PHOTO

After an oil spill, volunteers try to capture oil-covered penguins. The oil affects the penguins' ability to float. So, oil-covered penguins often won't go into the water to get food. The penguins may also swallow oil, harming their stomach, kidneys, and lungs. Once captured, the penguins are fed activated charcoal. The charcoal helps the penguins get rid of any oil they have swallowed. Then, the birds are washed to remove oil from their feathers.

PRE-READING ACTIVITY

FOLDNOTES **Two-Panel Flip Chart**
Before you read the chapter, create the FoldNote entitled "Two-Panel Flip Chart" described in the **Study Skills** section of the Appendix. Label the flaps of the two-panel flip chart with "Environmental problems" and "Environmental solutions." As you read the chapter, write information you learn about each category under the appropriate flap.

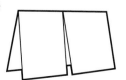

START-UP ACTIVITY

Recycling Paper

In this activity, you will be making paper without cutting down trees. You will be reusing paper that has already been made.

Procedure

1. Tear **two sheets of old newspaper** into small pieces, and put them in a **blender**. Add **1 L of water**. Cover and blend until the mixture is soupy.

2. Fill a **square pan** with **water** to a depth of 2 cm to 3 cm. Place a **wire screen** in the pan. Pour 250 mL of the paper mixture onto the screen, and spread the mixture evenly.

3. Lift the screen out of the water with the paper on it. Drain excess water into the pan.

4. Place the screen inside a **section of newspaper**. Close the newspaper, and turn it over so that the screen is on top of the paper mixture.

5. Cover the newspaper with a **flat board**. Press on the board to squeeze out excess water.

6. Open the newspaper, and let your paper mixture dry overnight. Use your recycled paper to write a note to a friend!

Analysis

1. How is your paper like regular paper? How is it different?

2. What could you do to improve your papermaking methods?

pollution an unwanted change in the environment caused by substances or forms of energy

Environmental Problems

Maybe you've heard warnings about dirty air, water, and soil. Or you've heard about the destruction of rain forests. Do these warnings mean our environment is in trouble?

In the late 1700s, the Industrial Revolution began. People started to rely more and more on machines. As a result, more harmful substances entered the air, water, and soil.

Pollution

Today, machines don't produce as much pollution as they once did. But there are more sources of pollution today than there once were. **Pollution** is an unwanted change in the environment caused by substances, such as wastes, or forms of energy, such as radiation. Anything that causes pollution is called a *pollutant*. Some pollutants are produced by natural events, such as volcanic eruptions. Many pollutants are human-made. Pollutants may harm plants, animals, and humans.

Garbage

The average American throws away more trash than the average person in any other nation—about 12 kg of trash a week. This trash often goes to a landfill like the one in **Figure 1.** Other landfills contain medical waste, lead paint, and other hazardous wastes. *Hazardous waste* includes wastes that can catch fire; corrode, or eat through metal; explode; or make people sick. Many industries, such as paper mills and oil refineries, produce hazardous wastes.

✓ **Reading Check** What is hazardous waste? (*See the Appendix for answers to Reading Checks.*)

Figure 1 *Every year, Americans throw away about 200 million metric tons of garbage.*

Figure 2 *Fertilizer promotes the growth of algae. As algae become overpopulated, die, and decompose, oxygen in the water is used up. So, fish die because they cannot get oxygen.*

Chemicals

People need and use many chemicals. Some chemicals are used to treat diseases. Other chemicals are used in plastics and preserved foods. Sometimes, the same chemicals that help people may harm the environment. As shown in **Figure 2,** fertilizers and pesticides may pollute soil and water.

CFCs and PCBs are two groups of harmful chemicals. Ozone protects Earth from harmful ultraviolet light. CFCs destroy ozone. CFCs were used in aerosols, refrigerators, and plastics. The second group, PCBs, was once used in appliances and paints. PCBs are poisonous and may cause cancer. Today, the use of CFCs and PCBs is banned. But CFCs are still found in the atmosphere. And PCBs are still found in even the most remote areas on Earth.

High-Powered Wastes

Nuclear power plants provide electricity to many homes and businesses. The plants also produce radioactive wastes. *Radioactive wastes* are hazardous wastes that give off radiation. Some of these wastes take thousands of years to become harmless.

Gases

Earth's atmosphere is made up of a mixture of gases, including carbon dioxide. The atmosphere acts as a protective blanket. It keeps Earth warm enough for life to exist. Since the Industrial Revolution, however, the amount of carbon dioxide in the atmosphere has increased. Carbon dioxide and other air pollutants act like a greenhouse, trapping heat around the Earth. Many scientists think the increase in carbon dioxide has increased global temperatures. If temperatures continue to rise, the polar icecaps could melt. Then, the level of the world's oceans would rise. Coastal areas could flood as a result.

CONNECTION TO Chemistry

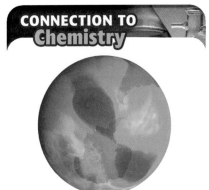

Ozone Holes This image of two holes in the ozone layer (the purple areas over Antarctica) was taken in 2002. Ozone in the stratosphere absorbs most of the ultraviolet light that comes from the sun. Ozone is destroyed by CFCs. Research how CFCs destroy ozone. Make a model demonstrating this process. Then, identify the effects of too much ultraviolet light.

ACTIVITY

renewable resource a natural resource that can be replaced at the same rate at which the resource is consumed

nonrenewable resource a resource that forms at a rate that is much slower than the rate at which it is consumed

Figure 3 *This area has been mined for iron using a method called* strip mining.

Noise

Some pollutants affect the senses. These pollutants include loud noises. Too much noise is not just annoying. Noise pollution affects your ability to hear and think clearly. And it may damage your hearing. People who work in noisy environments, such as in construction zones, must protect their ears.

Resource Depletion

Some of Earth's resources are renewable. But other resources are nonrenewable. A **renewable resource** is one that can be replaced at the same rate at which the resource is used. Solar and wind energy are renewable resources, as are some kinds of trees. A **nonrenewable resource** is one that cannot be replaced or that can be replaced only over thousands or millions of years. Most minerals and fossil fuels, such as oil and coal, are nonrenewable resources.

Nonrenewable resources cannot last forever. These resources will become more expensive as they become harder to find. The removal of some materials from the Earth also carries a high price tag. This removal may lead to oil spills, loss of habitat, and damage from mining, as shown in **Figure 3.**

Renewable or Nonrenewable?

Some resources once thought to be renewable are becoming nonrenewable. For example, scientists used to think that fresh water was a renewable resource. However, in some areas, water supplies are being used faster than they are being replaced. Eventually, these areas may run out of fresh water. So, scientists are working on ways to keep these water supplies from being used up.

14 Concept Mapping Use the following terms to create a concept map: *pollution, radioactive wastes, gases, pollutants, CFCs, PCBs, hazardous wastes, chemicals, noise,* and *garbage.*

15 Analyzing Ideas How may deforestation have contributed to the extinction of some species?

16 Predicting Consequences Imagine that the supply of fossil fuels is going to run out in 50 years. What will happen if people are not prepared when the supply runs out? What might be done to prepare for such an event?

17 Evaluating Conclusions A scientist thinks that farms should be planted with many different kinds of crops instead of a single crop. Based on what you learned about biodiversity, evaluate the scientist's conclusion. What problems might this cause?

18 Applying Concepts Imagine that a new species has moved into a local habitat. The species feeds on some of the same plants that the native species do, but it has no natural predators. Describe what might happen to local habitats as a result.

19 Making Inferences Many scientists think that forests are nonrenewable resources. Explain why they might have this opinion.

The line graph below shows the concentration of carbon dioxide in the atmosphere between 1958 and 1994. Use this graph to answer the questions that follow.

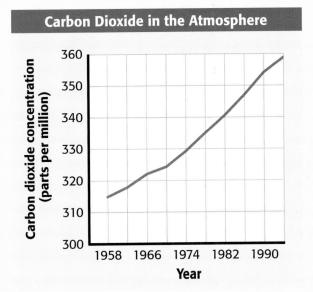

Carbon Dioxide in the Atmosphere

20 What was the concentration of carbon dioxide in parts per million in 1960? in 1994?

21 What is the average change in carbon dioxide concentration every 4 years?

22 If the concentration of carbon dioxide continues to change at the rate shown in the graph, what will the concentration be in 2010?

Standardized Test Preparation

Read the passages below. Then, answer the questions that follow each passage.

Passage 1 The scientist woke up and jogged over to the rain forest. There she observed the water-recycling experiment. She took a swim in the ocean, after which she walked through a mangrove forest on her way home. At home, she ate lunch and went to the computer lab. From the lab, she could monitor the sensors that would alert her if any part of the ecosystem failed to cycle properly. This monitoring was very important to the scientist and her research team because their lives depended on the health of their sealed environment.

1. Based on the passage, the reader can conclude which of the following?
   A The scientist lives in an artificial environment.
   B The scientist lives by herself.
   C The scientist and her research team are studying a newly discovered island.
   D The scientist does not rely on the health of her environment.

2. Which of the following statements is a fact in the passage?
   F The scientist is scared that her environment is being destroyed.
   G The scientist depends on sensors to alert her to trouble.
   H The scientist lives in an open environment.
   I The scientist eats lunch at home every day.

3. Based on the passage, which of the following events happened first?
   A The scientist walked through the mangrove forest.
   B The scientist checked the water-recycling experiment.
   C The scientist swam in the ocean.
   D The scientist ate lunch.

Passage 2 All along the Gulf Coast, marine scientists and Earth scientists are trying to find methods to reduce or eliminate the dead zone. They have made models of the Mississippi River ecosystem that have accurately predicted the data that have since been collected. The scientists have changed the models to see what happens. For example, wetlands are one of nature's best filters. Wetlands take up a lot of the chemicals present in water. Scientists predict that adding wetlands to the Mississippi River watershed could reduce the chemicals reaching the Gulf of Mexico, possibly reducing the dead zone.

1. Based on the passage, what can you conclude about the dead zone?
   A It is found in the Mississippi River.
   B It may be prevented by adding wetlands to the Mississippi River watershed.
   C It reduces the chemicals reaching the Gulf of Mexico.
   D It is not caused by chemicals.

2. Based on the passage, which of the following statements about models is true?
   F Models do not accurately predict data.
   G Scientists do not change models.
   H Scientists use models to make predictions.
   I Models are always used for research.

3. Based on the passage, why did the scientists change their models?
   A to predict the effects of adding wetlands to the Mississippi River watershed
   B to find out why the dead zone happened
   C to eliminate the dead zone
   D to predict why there are a lot of chemicals in the Gulf of Mexico

The table below shows the change in ozone levels between 1960 and 1990 above Halley Bay, Antarctica. Use the table to answer the questions that follow.

October Ozone Levels Above Halley Bay, Antarctica, in Dobson Units (DU)	
Year	Ozone level (DU)
1960	300
1970	280
1980	235
1990	190

1. According to the table, which of the following is the most likely ozone level for October 2000?

A 120 DU

B 150 DU

C 235 DU

D 280 DU

2. According to the table, the ozone level above Halley Bay is doing which of the following?

F It steadily increased between 1960 and 1990.

G It fell by 37% between 1960 and 1990.

H It decreased by an average of 37 DU per year.

I It decreased by about 25% every 10 years.

3. What is the percent decrease in ozone level between 1980 and 1990?

A 16%

B 19%

C 24%

D 81%

4. What is the average loss of ozone level per year in DU?

F 4 DU

G 6 DU

H 37 DU

I 63 DU

Read each question below, and choose the best answer.

1. About 15 m of topsoil covers the western plains of the United States. If topsoil forms at the rate of 2.5 cm per 500 years, how long did it take for 15 m of topsoil to form?

A 3,000 years

B 7,500 years

C 18,750 years

D 300,000 years

2. The dimensions of a habitat are 16 km by 6 km. If these dimensions are decreased by 50%, what will the area of the habitat be?

F 22 km^2

G 24 km^2

H 48 km^2

I 96 km^2

3. If each person in a city of 500,000 people throws away 12 kg of trash each week, how many metric tons of trash does the city produce per year? (There are 1,000 kg in a metric ton.)

A 6,000 metric tons

B 26,000 metric tons

C 312,000 metric tons

D 312,000,000 metric tons

4. Producing one ton of new glass creates about 175 kg of mining waste. Using 50% recycled glass cuts this rate by 75%. Which of the following equations calculates y, the mass of mining waste produced using 50% recycled glass?

F $y = 175 \times 0.25$

G $y = 175 \times 0.75$

H $y = 175 \times 0.5$

I $y = 175 \div 0.75$

Standardized Test Preparation

Science in Action

Scientific Debate

Where Should the Wolves Roam?

The U.S. Fish and Wildlife Service once listed the gray wolf as an endangered species and devised a plan to reintroduce the wolf to parts of the U.S. The goal was to establish a population of at least 100 wolves at each location. In April 2003, gray wolves were reclassified as a threatened species in much of the United States. Eventually, gray wolves may be removed from the endangered species list entirely. But some ranchers and hunters are uneasy about the reintroduction of gray wolves, and some environmentalists and wolf enthusiasts think the plan doesn't go far enough to protect wolves.

Math ACTiViTy

Scientists tried to establish a population of 100 wolves in Idaho. But the population grew to 285 wolves. By what percentage did the population exceed expectations?

Science, Technology, and Society

Hydrogen-Fueled Automobiles

Can you imagine a car that purrs quieter than a kitten and gives off water vapor instead of harmful pollutants? These cars may sound like science fiction. But such cars already exist! They run on one of the most common elements in the world—hydrogen. Some car companies are already speculating that one day all cars will run on hydrogen. The U.S. government has also taken notice. In 2003, President George W. Bush promised $1.2 billion to help research and develop hydrogen-fueled cars.

Language Arts ACTiViTy

WRITING SKILL Research hydrogen-fueled cars. Then, write a letter to a car company, your senator, or the President expressing your opinion about the development of hydrogen-fueled cars.

Phil McCrory

Hairy Oil Spills Phil McCrory, a hairdresser in Huntsville, Alabama, asked a brilliant question when he saw an otter whose fur was drenched with oil from the *Exxon Valdez* oil spill. If the otter's fur soaked up all the oil, why wouldn't human hair do the same? McCrory gathered hair from the floor of his salon and took it home to perform his own experiments. He stuffed hair into a pair of his wife's pantyhose and tied the ankles together to form a bagel-shaped bundle. McCrory floated the bundle in his son's wading pool and poured used motor oil into the center of the ring. When he pulled the ring closed, not a drop of oil remained in the water!

McCrory approached the National Aeronautics and Space Administration (NASA) with his discovery. Based on tests performed by NASA, scientists estimated that 64 million kilograms of hair in reusable mesh pillows could have cleaned up all of the oil spilled by the *Exxon Valdez* within a week! Unfortunately, the $2 billion spent on the cleanup removed only about 12% of the oil.

Social Studies ACTiViTY

Make a map of an oil spill. Show the areas that were affected. Indicate some of the animal populations affected by the spill, such as penguins.

To learn more about these Science in Action topics, visit go.hrw.com and type in the keyword HL5ENVF.

Current Science

Check out Current Science® articles related to this chapter by visiting go.hrw.com. Just type in the keyword HL5CS21.

Energy Resources

The Big Idea

Sources of energy differ in quantity, distribution, usefulness, and the time required for formation.

SECTION

1 Natural Resources 102

2 Fossil Fuels 106

3 Alternative Resources 114

About the PHOTO

Would you believe that this house is made from empty soda cans and old tires? Well, it is! *The Castle,* named by its designer, architect Mike Reynolds, and located in Taos, New Mexico, not only uses recycled materials but also saves Earth's energy resources. All of the energy used to run this house comes directly from the sun, and the water used for household activities is rainwater.

PRE-READING ACTIVITY

Graphic Organizer

Comparison Table Before you read the chapter, create the graphic organizer entitled "Comparison Table" described in the **Study Skills** section of the Appendix. Label the columns with an energy resource from the chapter. Label the rows with "Pros" and "Cons." As you read the chapter, fill in the table with details about the pros and cons of each energy resource.

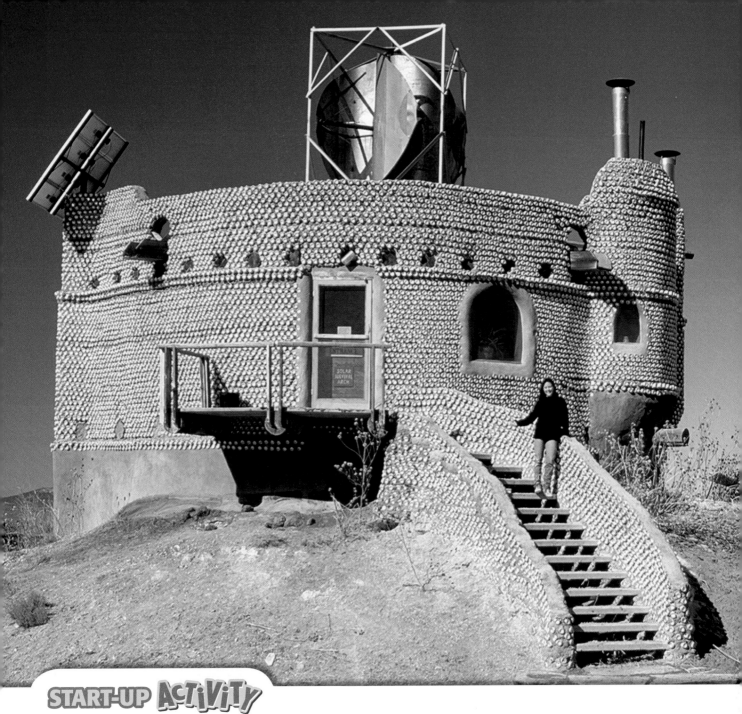

START-UP ACTIVITY

What Is the Sun's Favorite Color?

Try the following activity to see which colors are better than others at absorbing the sun's energy.

Procedure

1. Obtain **at least five balloons** that are different colors but the same size and shape. One of the balloons should be white, and one should be black. Do not inflate the balloons.

2. Place **several small ice cubes** in each balloon. Each balloon should contain the same amount of ice.

3. Line up the balloons on a flat, uniformly colored surface that receives direct sunlight. Make sure that all of the balloons receive the same amount of sunlight and that the openings in the balloons are not facing directly toward the sun.

4. Record the time that it takes the ice to melt completely in each of the balloons. You can tell how much ice has melted in each balloon by pinching the balloons open and then gently squeezing the balloon.

Analysis

1. In which balloon did the ice melt first? Why?

2. What color would you paint a device used to collect solar energy? Explain your answer.

Natural Resources

What does the water you drink, the paper you write on, the gasoline used in the cars you ride in, and the air you breathe have in common?

Water, trees used to make paper, crude oil used to make gasoline, and air are just a few examples of Earth's resources. Can you think of other examples of Earth's resources?

What You Will Learn

- Describe how humans use natural resources.
- Compare renewable resources with nonrenewable resources.
- Explain three ways that humans can conserve natural resources.

Vocabulary

natural resource
renewable resource
nonrenewable resource
recycling

READING STRATEGY

Reading Organizer As you read this section, make a concept map by using the terms above.

Earth's Resources

The Earth provides almost everything needed for life. For example, the Earth's atmosphere provides the air you breathe, maintains air temperatures, and produces rain. The oceans and other waters of the Earth give you food and needed water. The solid part of the Earth gives nutrients, such as potassium, to the plants you eat. These resources that the Earth provides for you are called natural resources.

A **natural resource** is any natural material that is used by humans. Examples of natural resources are water, petroleum, minerals, forests, and animals. Most resources are changed and made into products that make people's lives more comfortable and convenient, as shown in **Figure 1.** The energy we get from many of these resources, such as gasoline and wind, ultimately comes from the sun's energy.

Figure 1 **Natural Resources**

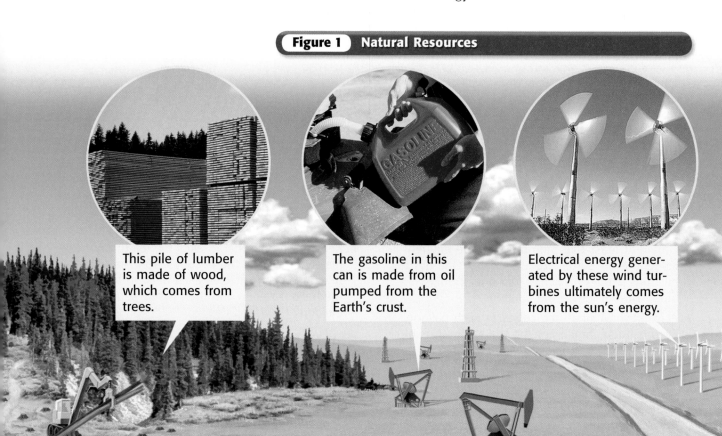

This pile of lumber is made of wood, which comes from trees.

The gasoline in this can is made from oil pumped from the Earth's crust.

Electrical energy generated by these wind turbines ultimately comes from the sun's energy.

Renewable Resources

Some natural resources can be renewed. A **renewable resource** is a natural resource that can be replaced at the same rate at which the resource is used. **Figure 2** shows two examples of renewable resources. Although many resources are renewable, they still can be used up before they can be renewed. Trees, for example, are renewable. However, some forests are being cut down faster than new forests can grow to replace them.

✓ Reading Check What is a renewable resource? (*See the Appendix for answers to Reading Checks.*)

Nonrenewable Resources

Not all of Earth's natural resources are renewable. A **nonrenewable resource** is a resource that forms at a rate that is much slower than the rate at which it is consumed. Coal, shown in **Figure 3,** is an example of a nonrenewable resource. It takes millions of years for coal to form. Once coal is used up, it is no longer available. Petroleum and natural gas are other examples of nonrenewable resources. When these resources become scarce, humans will have to find other resources to replace them.

Figure 2 *Trees and fresh water are just a few of the renewable resources available on Earth.*

natural resource any natural material that is used by humans, such as water, petroleum, minerals, forests, and animals

renewable resource a natural resource that can be replaced at the same rate at which the resource is consumed

nonrenewable resource a resource that forms at a rate that is much slower than the rate at which it is consumed

Figure 3 *The coal used in the industrial process shown here is not quickly replaced by natural processes.*

Conserving Natural Resources

Whether the natural resources you use are renewable or nonrenewable, you should be careful how you use them. To conserve natural resources, you should try to use them only when necessary. For example, leaving the faucet on while brushing your teeth wastes clean water. Turning the faucet on only to rinse your brush saves water that you may need for other uses.

Conserving resources also means taking care of the resources even when you are not using them. For example, it is important to keep lakes, rivers, and other water resources free of pollution. Polluted lakes and rivers can affect the water you drink. Also, polluted water resources can harm the plants and animals, including humans, that depend on them to survive.

Energy Conservation

The energy we use to heat our homes, drive our cars, and run our computers comes from natural resources. The way in which we choose to use energy on a daily basis affects the availability of the natural resources. Most of the natural resources that provide us energy are nonrenewable resources. So, if we don't limit our use of energy now, the resources may not be available in the future.

As with all natural resources, conserving energy is important. You can conserve energy by being careful to use only the resources that you need. For example, turn lights off when you are not using them. And make sure the washing machine is full before you start it, as shown in **Figure 4.** You can also ride a bike, walk, or take a bus because these methods use fewer resources than a car does.

Figure 4 *Making sure the washing machine is full before running it is one way you can avoid wasting natural resources.*

Reduce, Reuse, Recycle

Another way to conserve natural resources is to recycle, as shown in **Figure 5. Recycling** is the process of reusing materials from waste or scrap. Recycling reduces the amount of natural resources that must be obtained from the Earth. For example, recycling paper reduces the number of trees that must be cut down to make new paper products. Recycling also conserves energy. Though energy is required to recycle materials, it takes less energy to recycle an aluminum can than it does to make a new one!

Newspaper, aluminum cans, most plastic containers, and cardboard boxes can be recycled. Most plastic containers have a number on them. This number informs you whether the item can be recycled. Plastic products with the numbers 1 and 2 can be recycled in most communities. Check with your community's recycling center to see what kinds of materials the center recycles.

recycling the process of recovering valuable or useful materials from waste or scrap; the process of reusing some items

Figure 5 *You can recycle many household items to help conserve natural resources.*

✓ **Reading Check** What are some kinds of products that can be recycled?

SECTION Review

Summary

● We use natural resources such as water, petroleum, and lumber to make our lives more comfortable and convenient.

● Renewable resources can be replaced within a relatively short period of time, but nonrenewable resources may take thousands or even millions of years to form.

● Natural resources can be conserved by using only what is needed, taking care of resources, and recycling.

Using Key Terms

1. Use each of the following terms in a separate sentence: *natural resource, renewable resource, nonrenewable resource,* and *recycling.*

Understanding Key Ideas

2. How do humans use most natural resources?

3. Which of the following is a renewable resource?
   a. oil
   b. water
   c. coal
   d. natural gas

4. Describe three ways to conserve natural resources.

Math Skills

5. If a faucet dripped for 8.6 h and 3.3 L of water dripped out every hour, how many liters of water dripped out altogether?

Critical Thinking

6. **Making Inferences** How does human activity affect Earth's renewable and nonrenewable resources?

7. **Applying Concepts** List five products you regularly use that can be recycled.

8. **Making Inferences** Why is the availability of some renewable resources more of a concern now than it was 100 years ago?

Fossil Fuels

How does a sunny day 200 million years ago relate to your life today?

Chances are that if you traveled to school today or used a product made of plastic, you used some of the energy from sunlight that fell on Earth several hundred million years ago. Life as you know it would be very different without the fuels or products formed from plants and animals that lived alongside the dinosaurs.

Energy Resources

The fuels we use to run cars, ships, planes, and factories and to generate electrical energy, shown in **Figure 1,** are energy resources. *Energy resources* are natural resources that humans use to generate energy. Most of the energy we use comes from a group of natural resources called fossil fuels. A **fossil fuel** is a nonrenewable energy resource formed from the remains of plants and animals that lived long ago. Examples of fossil fuels include petroleum, coal, and natural gas.

Energy is released from fossil fuels when they are burned. For example, the energy from burning coal in a power plant is used to produce electrical energy. However, because fossil fuels are a nonrenewable resource, once they are burned, they are gone. Therefore, like other resources, fossil fuels need to be conserved. In the 21st century, societies will continue to explore alternatives to fossil fuels. But they will also focus on developing more-efficient ways to use these fuels.

What You Will Learn

- Describe what energy resources are.
- Identify three different forms of fossil fuels.
- Explain how fossil fuels form.
- Describe how fossil fuels are found and obtained.
- Identify four problems with fossil fuels.

Vocabulary

fossil fuel	coal
petroleum	acid precipitation
natural gas	smog

READING STRATEGY

Brainstorming The key idea of this section is fossil fuels. Brainstorm words and phrases related to fossil fuels.

fossil fuel a nonrenewable energy resource formed from the remains of organisms that lived long ago; examples include oil, coal, and natural gas

Figure 1 *Light produced from electrical energy can be seen in this satellite image taken from space.*

Figure 2 *Some refineries use a process called* distillation *to separate petroleum into various types of petroleum products.*

Types of Fossil Fuels

All living things are made up of the element carbon. Because fossil fuels are formed from the remains of plants and animals, all fossil fuels are made of carbon, too. Most of the carbon in fossil fuels exists as hydrogen-carbon compounds called *hydrocarbons*. But different fossil fuels have different forms. Fossil fuels may exist as liquids, gases, or solids.

Liquid Fossil Fuels: Petroleum

A liquid mixture of complex hydrocarbon compounds is called **petroleum.** Petroleum is also commonly known as *crude oil*. Petroleum is separated into several kinds of products in refineries, such as the one shown in **Figure 2.** Examples of fossil fuels separated from petroleum are gasoline, jet fuel, kerosene, diesel fuel, and fuel oil.

More than 40% of the world's energy comes from petroleum products. Petroleum products are the main fuel for forms of transportation, such as airplanes, trains, boats, and ships. Crude oil is so valuable that it is often called *black gold*.

Gaseous Fossil Fuels: Natural Gas

A gaseous mixture of hydrocarbons is called **natural gas.** Most natural gas is used for heating, but it is also used for generating electrical energy. Your kitchen stove may be powered by natural gas. Some motor vehicles, such as the van in **Figure 3,** use natural gas as fuel. An advantage of using natural gas is that using it causes less air pollution than using oil does. However, natural gas is very flammable. Gas leaks can lead to fires or deadly explosions.

Methane, CH_4, is the main component of natural gas. But other components, such as butane and propane, can be separated from natural gas, too. Butane and propane are often used as fuel for camp stoves and outdoor grills.

✓ Reading Check What is natural gas most often used for? (*See the Appendix for answers to Reading Checks.*)

petroleum a liquid mixture of complex hydrocarbon compounds; used widely as a fuel source

natural gas a mixture of gaseous hydrocarbons located under the surface of the Earth, often near petroleum deposits; used as a fuel

Figure 3 *Vehicles powered by natural gas are becoming more common.*

Figure 4 *This coal is being gathered so that it may be burned in the power plant shown in the background.*

coal a fossil fuel that forms underground from partially decomposed plant material

Solid Fossil Fuels: Coal

The solid fossil fuel that humans use most is coal. **Coal** is a fossil fuel that is formed underground from partially decomposed plant material. Coal was once the major source of energy in the United States. People burned coal in stoves to heat their homes. They also used coal in transportation. Many trains in the 1800s and early 1900s were powered by coal-burning steam locomotives.

As cleaner energy resources became available, people reduced their use of coal. People began to use coal less because burning coal produces large amounts of air pollution. Now, people use forms of transportation that use oil instead of coal as fuel. In the United States, coal is now rarely used as a fuel for heating. However, many power plants, such as the one shown in **Figure 4,** burn coal to generate electrical energy.

✔ **Reading Check** In the 1800s and early 1900s, what was coal most commonly used for?

For another activity related to this chapter, go to **go.hrw.com** and type in the keyword **HZ5ENRW.**

CONNECTION TO Chemistry

Hydrocarbons Both petroleum and natural gas are made of compounds called *hydrocarbons*. A hydrocarbon is an organic compound that contains only carbon and hydrogen. A molecule of propane, C_3H_8, a gaseous fossil fuel, contains three carbons and eight hydrogens. Using a molecular model set, create a model of a propane molecule. (Hint: Each carbon atom should have four bonds, and each hydrogen atom should have one bond.)

ACTIVITY

How Do Fossil Fuels Form?

All fossil fuels form from the buried remains of ancient organisms. But different kinds of fossil fuels form in different ways and from different kinds of organisms.

Petroleum and Natural Gas Formation

Petroleum and natural gas form mainly from the remains of microscopic sea organisms. When these organisms die, their remains settle on the ocean floor. There, the remains are buried in sediment. Over time, the sediment is compacted and slowly becomes rock. Through physical and chemical changes over millions of years, the remains of the organisms become petroleum and gas. Gradually, more rocks form above the rocks that contain the fossil fuels. Under the pressure of overlying rocks and sediments, the fossil fuels can move through permeable rocks. *Permeable rocks* are rocks through which fluids, such as petroleum and gas, can move. As shown in **Figure 5,** these permeable rocks become reservoirs that hold petroleum and natural gas.

The formation of petroleum and natural gas is an ongoing process. Part of the remains of today's sea life will become petroleum and natural gas millions of years from now.

Rock Sponge

1. Place **samples of sandstone, limestone,** and **shale** in separate **Petri dishes.**
2. Place **five drops of light machine oil** on each rock sample.
3. Observe and record the time required for the oil to be absorbed by each of the rock samples.
4. Which rock sample absorbed the oil fastest? Why?
5. Based on your findings, describe a property that allows fossil fuels to be easily removed from reservoir rock.

Figure 5 *Petroleum and gas move through permeable rock. Eventually, these fuels are collected in reservoirs. Rocks that are folded upward are excellent fossil-fuel traps.*

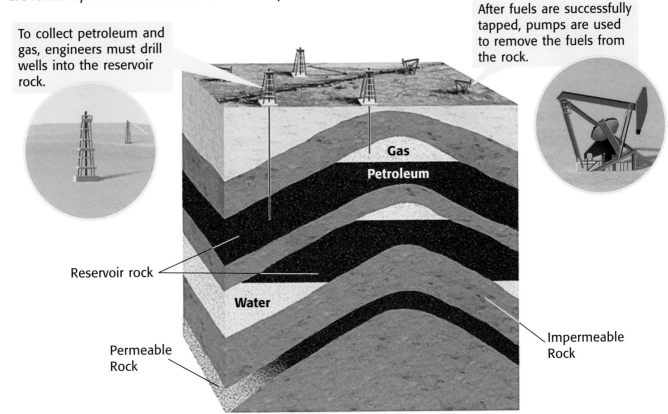

To collect petroleum and gas, engineers must drill wells into the reservoir rock.

After fuels are successfully tapped, pumps are used to remove the fuels from the rock.

Gas

Petroleum

Reservoir rock

Water

Permeable Rock

Impermeable Rock

Coal Formation

Coal forms underground over millions of years when pressure and heat cause changes in the remains of swamp plants. When these plants die, they sink to the bottom of the swamp. If they do not decay completely, coal formation may begin. The stages of coal formation are shown in **Figure 6.**

The first step of the process is the change of plant remains into peat. Peat is brown, crumbly matter made mostly of plant material and water. Peat is not coal. But, in some parts of the world, peat is dried and burned for heat or as fuel. If the peat is buried by sediment, pressure and heat are applied to the peat, and coal begins to form. The pressure and heat force water and gases out of the coal. As a result, the coal becomes harder, and its carbon content increases. The amount of heat and pressure determines the type of coal that forms. Lignite forms first, followed by bituminous coal, and, finally, anthracite. Coal formation can stop during any part of this process. Today, all three types of coal are mined throughout the world. The greater the carbon content of the coal is, the more cleanly the coal burns. But when burned, all types of coal pollute the air.

Figure 6 **Coal Formation**

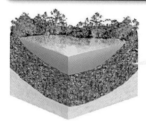

Stage 1: Peat Forms
Sunken swamp plants that have not decayed completely can change into peat. About 60% of an average sample of dried peat is carbon.

Stage 2: Lignite Forms
If sediment buries the peat, pressure and temperature increase. The peat slowly changes into a type of coal called *lignite.* Lignite is harder than peat is, and about 70% of an average sample of lignite is carbon.

Stage 3: Bituminous Coal Forms
If more sediment is added, pressure and temperature force more water and gases out of the lignite. Lignite slowly changes into bituminous coal. About 80% of an average sample of bituminous coal is carbon.

Stage 4: Anthracite Forms
If more sediment accumulates, temperature and pressure continue to increase. Bituminous coal slowly changes into anthracite. Anthracite is the hardest type of coal. About 90% of an average sample of anthracite is carbon.

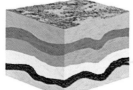

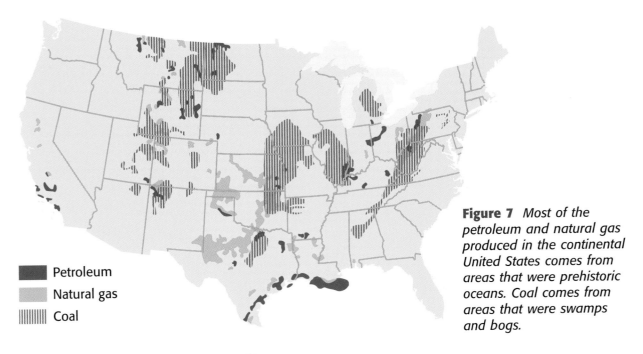

Petroleum

Natural gas

||||||| Coal

Figure 7 *Most of the petroleum and natural gas produced in the continental United States comes from areas that were prehistoric oceans. Coal comes from areas that were swamps and bogs.*

Where Are Fossil Fuels Found?

Fossil fuels are found in many parts of the world. Some fossil fuels are found on land, while other fossil fuels are found beneath the ocean. As shown in **Figure 7,** the United States has large reserves of petroleum, natural gas, and coal. Despite its large reserves of petroleum, the United States imports petroleum as well. About one-half of the petroleum used by the United States is imported from the Middle East, South America, Africa, Canada, and Mexico.

How Do We Obtain Fossil Fuels?

Humans use several methods to remove fossil fuels from the Earth's crust. The kind and location of fuel determine the method used to remove the fuel. People remove petroleum and natural gas from Earth by drilling wells into rock that contains these resources. Oil wells exist on land and in the ocean. For offshore drilling, engineers mount drills on platforms that are secured to the ocean floor or that float at the ocean's surface. **Figure 8** shows an offshore oil rig.

People obtain coal either by mining deep beneath Earth's surface or by surface mining. Surface mining, also known as *strip mining,* is the process by which soil and rock are stripped from the Earth's surface to expose the underlying coal that is to be mined.

Reading Check How are natural gas and petroleum removed from Earth?

Figure 8 *Large oil rigs, some of which are more than 300 m tall, operate offshore in many places, such as the Gulf of Mexico and the North Sea.*

1994

1935

Figure 9 *Notice how this statue looked before the effects of acid precipitation.*

acid precipitation precipitation, such as rain, sleet, or snow, that contains a high concentration of acids, often because of the pollution of the atmosphere

smog photochemical haze that forms when sunlight acts on industrial pollutants and burning fuels

Problems with Fossil Fuels

Although fossil fuels provide the energy we need, the methods of obtaining and using them can have negative effects on the environment. For example, when coal is burned without pollution controls, sulfur dioxide is released. Sulfur dioxide combines with moisture in the air to produce sulfuric acid. Sulfuric acid is one of the acids in acid precipitation. **Acid precipitation** is rain, sleet, or snow that has a high concentration of acids, often because of air pollutants. Acid precipitation negatively affects wildlife, plants, buildings, and statues, as shown in **Figure 9.**

✓ **Reading Check**   How can the burning of fossil fuels affect rain?

Coal Mining

The mining of coal can also create environmental problems. Surface mining removes soil, which some plants need for growth and some animals need for shelter. If land is not properly restored afterward, surface mining can destroy wildlife habitats. Coal mining can also lower water tables and pollute water supplies. The potential for underground mines to collapse endangers the lives of miners.

Petroleum Problems

Producing, transporting, and using petroleum can cause environmental problems and endanger wildlife. In June 2000, the carrier, *Treasure,* sank off the coast of South Africa and spilled more than 400 tons of oil. The toxic oil coated thousands of blackfooted penguins, as shown in **Figure 10.** The oil hindered the penguins from swimming and catching fish for food.

Smog

Burning petroleum products causes an environmental problem called smog. **Smog** is photochemical haze that forms when sunlight acts on industrial pollutants and burning fuels. Smog is particularly serious in cities such as Houston and Los Angeles as a result of millions of automobiles that burn gasoline. Also, mountains that surround Los Angeles prevent the wind from blowing pollutants away.

Figure 10 *The oil spilled from the carrier,* Treasure, *endangered the lives of many animals including the blackfooted penguins.*

Summary

- Energy resources are resources that humans use to produce energy.
- Petroleum is a liquid fossil fuel that is made of hydrocarbon compounds.
- Natural gas is a gaseous fossil fuel that is made of hydrocarbon compounds.
- Coal is a solid fossil fuel that forms from the remains of swamp plants.
- Petroleum and natural gas form from the remains of microscopic sea life.

- Fossil fuels are found all over the world. The United States imports half of the petroleum it uses from the Middle East, South America, Africa, Mexico, and Canada.
- Fossil fuels are obtained by drilling oil wells, mining below Earth's surface, and strip mining.
- Acid precipitation, smog, water pollution, and the destruction of wildlife habitat are some of the environmental problems that are created by the use of fossil fuels.

Using Key Terms

1. Use each of the following terms in a separate sentence: *energy resource, fossil fuel, petroleum, natural gas, coal, acid precipitation,* and *smog.*

Understanding Key Ideas

2. Which of the following types of coal contains the highest carbon content?
   a. lignite
   b. anthracite
   c. peat
   d. bituminous coal

3. Name a solid fossil fuel, a liquid fossil fuel, and a gaseous fossil fuel.

4. Briefly describe how petroleum and natural gas form.

5. How do we obtain petroleum and natural gas?

6. Describe the advantages and disadvantages of fossil fuel use.

Critical Thinking

7. **Making Comparisons** What is the difference between the organic material from which coal forms and the organic material from which petroleum and natural gas form?

8. **Making Inferences** Why can't carpooling and using mass-transit systems eliminate the problems associated with fossil fuels?

Interpreting Graphics

Use the pie chart below to answer the questions that follow.

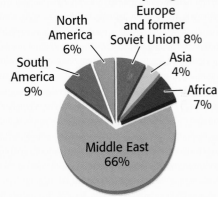

Oil Production by Region

North America 6%
Europe and former Soviet Union 8%
Asia 4%
Africa 7%
South America 9%
Middle East 66%

Source: International Energy Agency.

9. Which region produces the most oil?

10. If the total sales of oil in 2002 were $500 billion, what was the value of the oil produced in North America?

SCiLINKS

NSTA

Developed and maintained by the
National Science Teachers Association

For a variety of links related to this chapter, go to www.scilinks.org

Topic: Fossil Fuels
SciLinks code: HSM0614

Alternative Resources

What would your life be like if you couldn't play video games, turn on lights, microwave your dinner, take a hot shower, or take the bus to school?

Most of your energy needs and the energy needs of others are met by the use of fossil fuels. Yet, there are two main problems with fossil fuels. First, the availability of fossil fuels is limited. Fossil fuels are nonrenewable resources. Once fossil fuels are used up, new supplies won't be available for thousands—or even millions—of years.

Second, obtaining and using fossil fuels has environmental consequences. To continue to have access to energy and to overcome pollution, we must find alternative sources of energy.

Splitting the Atom: Fission

The energy released by a fission or fusion reaction is **nuclear energy.** *Fission* is a process in which the nuclei of radioactive atoms are split into two or more smaller nuclei, as shown in **Figure 1.** When fission takes place, a large amount of energy is released. This energy can be used to generate electrical energy. The SI unit for all forms of energy is the joule. However, electrical energy and nuclear energy is often measured in megawatts (MW).

What You Will Learn

● Describe alternatives to the use of fossil fuels.
● List advantages and disadvantages of using alternative energy resources.

Vocabulary

nuclear energy
chemical energy
solar energy
wind power
hydroelectric energy
biomass
gasohol
geothermal energy

READING STRATEGY

Paired Summarizing Read this section silently. In pairs, take turns summarizing the material. Stop to discuss ideas that seem confusing.

Figure 1 **Fission**

A neutron from a uranium-235 atom splits the nucleus into two smaller nuclei called *fission products* and two or more neutrons.

Uranium-235

Neutron

Neutron

Barium-142

Energy

Krypton-91

Pros and Cons of Fission

Nuclear power plants provide alternative sources of energy that do not have the problems that fossil fuels do. So, why don't we use nuclear energy more instead of using fossil fuels? Nuclear power plants produce dangerous radioactive wastes. Radioactive wastes must be removed from the plant and stored until their radioactivity decreases to a harmless level. But nuclear wastes can remain dangerously radioactive for thousands of years. These wastes must be stored in an isolated place where the radiation that they emit cannot harm anyone.

Another problem with nuclear power plants is the potential for accidental release of radiation into the environment. A release could happen if the plant overheats. If a plant's cooling system were to stop working, the plant would overheat. Then, its reactor could melt, and a large amount of radiation could escape into the environment. In addition, towers like the one shown in **Figure 2,** keep hot water from potentially disrupting the local ecosystem.

Figure 2 *Cooling towers are used to cool water leaving a nuclear power plant before the water is released into the environment.*

Combining Atoms: Fusion

Another method of getting energy from nuclei is fusion, shown in **Figure 3.** *Fusion* is the joining of two or more nuclei to form a larger nucleus. This process releases a large amount of energy and happens naturally in the sun.

The main advantage of fusion is that it produces few dangerous wastes. The main disadvantage of fusion is that very high temperatures are required for the reaction to take place. No known material can withstand such high temperatures. Therefore, the reaction must happen within a special environment, such as a magnetic field. Controlled fusion reactions have been limited to laboratory experiments.

nuclear energy the energy released by a fission or fusion reaction; the binding energy of the atomic nucleus

> ✓ **Reading Check** What is the advantage of producing energy through fusion? (*See the Appendix for answers to Reading Checks.*)

Figure 3 Fusion

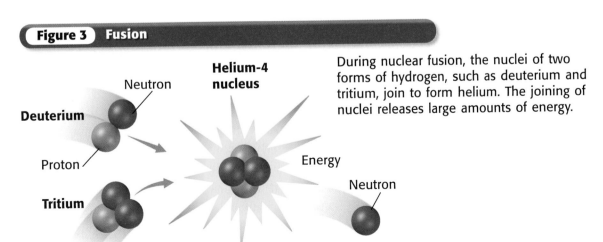

During nuclear fusion, the nuclei of two forms of hydrogen, such as deuterium and tritium, join to form helium. The joining of nuclei releases large amounts of energy.

Deuterium
Neutron
Helium-4 nucleus
Proton
Tritium
Energy
Neutron

Figure 4 *This image shows a prototype of a fuel-cell car. Power from fuel cells may be commonly used in the future.*

chemical energy the energy released when a chemical compound reacts to produce new compounds

solar energy the energy received by the Earth from the sun in the form of radiation

Chemical Energy

When you think of fuel for an automobile, you most likely think of gasoline. However, not all vehicles are fueled by gasoline. Some vehicles, such as the one shown in **Figure 4,** are powered by energy that is generated by fuel cells. Fuel cells power automobiles by converting **chemical energy** into electrical energy by reacting hydrogen and oxygen into water. One advantage of using fuel cells as energy sources is that fuel cells do not create pollution. The only byproduct of fuel cells is water. Fuel cells are also more efficient than internal combustion engines are.

The United States has been using fuel cells in space travel since the 1960s. Fuel cells have provided space crews with electrical energy and drinking water. One day, fuel-cell technology may be used to generate electrical energy in buildings, ships, and submarines, too.

CONNECTION TO Language Arts

WRITING SKILL **Resources of the Future** In 100 years do you think humans will still be using fossil fuels to power their cars? Maybe humans will be using alternative energy resources. Maybe humans won't even be driving cars! Write a short, creative, science fiction story describing the energy use of humans 100 years from now.

Solar Energy

Almost all forms of energy, such as the energy of fossil fuels, come from the sun. The energy received by the Earth from the sun in the form of radiation is **solar energy.** The Earth receives more than enough solar energy to meet all of our energy needs. And because the Earth continuously receives solar energy, this energy is a renewable resource. Solar energy can be used directly to heat buildings and to generate electrical energy. However, we do not yet have the technology to generate the amount of electrical energy we need from solar energy.

Sunlight can be changed into electrical energy through the use of solar cells or photovoltaic cells. You may have used a calculator that is powered by solar cells. *Solar panels* are large panels made up of many solar cells wired together. Solar panels mounted on the roofs of some homes and businesses provide some of the electrical energy used in the buildings.

✓ Reading Check Where does the energy of fossil fuels come from?

Solar Heating

Solar energy is also used for direct heating through solar collectors. *Solar collectors* are dark-colored boxes that have glass or plastic tops. A common use of solar collectors is to heat water, as shown in **Figure 5.** More than 1 million solar water heaters have been installed in the United States. Solar water heaters are especially common in Florida and California.

Pros and Cons of Solar Energy

One of the best things about solar energy is that it doesn't produce pollution. Also, solar energy is renewable, because it comes from the sun. However, some climates don't have enough sunny days to benefit from solar energy. Also, although solar energy is free, solar cells and solar collectors are more expensive to make than other energy systems are. The cost of installing a complete solar-power system in a house can be one-third of the total cost of the house.

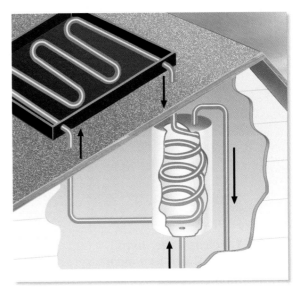

Figure 5 *The liquid in the solar collector is heated by the sun. Then, the liquid is pumped through tubes that run through a water heater, which causes the temperature of the water to increase.*

Wind Power

Wind is made indirectly by solar energy through the uneven heating of air. Energy can be harnessed from wind. **Wind power** is the use of a windmill to drive an electric generator. Clusters of wind turbines, like the ones shown in **Figure 6,** can generate a significant amount of electrical energy. Wind energy is renewable, and it doesn't cause any pollution. However, in many areas, the wind isn't strong enough or frequent enough to create energy on a large scale.

wind power the use of a windmill to drive an electric generator

Figure 6 *Wind turbines take up only a small part of the ground's surface. As a result, the land on wind farms can be used for more than one purpose.*

Figure 7 *Falling water turns water wheels, which turn giant millstones used to grind grain into flour.*

hydroelectric energy electrical energy produced by falling water

Figure 8 *Falling water turns turbines inside hydroelectric dams and generates electrical energy for millions of people.*

Hydroelectric Energy

Humans have used the energy of falling water for thousands of years. Water wheels, such as the one shown in **Figure 7,** have been around since ancient times. In the early years of the Industrial Revolution, water wheels provided energy for many factories. Today, the energy of falling water is used to generate electrical energy. Electrical energy produced by falling water is called **hydroelectric energy.**

Pros and Cons of Hydroelectric Energy

After the dam is built, hydroelectric energy is inexpensive and causes little pollution. It is renewable because water constantly cycles from water sources to the air, to the land, and back to the water source. But like wind energy, hydroelectric energy is not available everywhere. It can be produced only where large volumes of falling water can be harnessed. Huge dams, such as the one in **Figure 8,** must be built on major rivers to capture enough water to generate significant amounts of electrical energy.

Using more hydroelectric energy could reduce the demand for fossil fuels, but there are trade-offs. Building the large dams necessary for hydroelectric power plants often destroys other resources, such as forests and wildlife habitats. For example, hydroelectric dams on the lower Snake and Columbia Rivers in Washington state disrupt the migratory paths of local populations of salmon and steelhead. Large numbers of these fish die each year because their migratory path is disrupted. Dams can also decrease water quality and create erosion problems.

✓ Reading Check Why is hydroelectric energy renewable?

Power from Plants

Plants are similar to solar collectors. Both absorb energy from the sun and store it for later use. Leaves, wood, and other parts of plants contain the stored energy. Even the dung of plant-grazing animals is high in stored energy. These sources of energy are called biomass. **Biomass** is organic matter that can be a source of energy.

Burning Biomass

Biomass energy can be released in several ways. The most common way is to burn biomass. Approximately 70% of people living in developing countries, about half the world population, burn wood or charcoal to heat their homes and cook their food. In contrast, about 5% of the people in the United States heat and cook this way. Scientists estimate that the burning of wood and animal dung accounts for approximately 14% of the world's total energy use. **Figure 9** shows a woman who is preparing cow dung that will be dried and used for fuel.

Gasohol

Biomass material can also be changed into liquid fuel. Plants that contain sugar or starch can be made into alcohol. The alcohol can be burned as a fuel. Or alcohol can be mixed with gasoline to make a fuel called **gasohol.** More than 1,000 L of alcohol can be made from 1 acre of corn. But people in the United States use a large amount of fuel for their cars. And the alcohol produced from about 40% of one corn harvest in the United States would provide only 10% of the fuel used in our cars! Biomass is a renewable source of energy. However, producing biomass requires land that could be used for growing food.

biomass organic matter that can be a source of energy

gasohol a mixture of gasoline and alcohol that is used as a fuel

Miles per Acre

Imagine that you own a car that runs on alcohol made from corn that you grow. You drive your car about 15,000 mi per year, and you get 240 gal of alcohol from each acre of corn that you process. If your car has a gas mileage of 25 mi/gal, how many acres of corn must you process to fuel your car for a year?

Figure 9 *In many parts of the world where firewood is scarce, people burn animal dung for energy.*

Energy from Within Earth

If you have ever seen a volcanic eruption, you know how powerful the Earth can be. The energy produced by the heat within Earth is called **geothermal energy.**

geothermal energy the energy produced by heat within the Earth

Geothermal Energy

In some areas, groundwater is heated by *magma,* or melted rock. Often, the heated groundwater becomes steam. *Geysers* are natural vents that discharge this steam or water in a column into the air. The steam and hot water can also escape through wells drilled into the rock. From these wells, geothermal power plants can harness the energy from within Earth by pumping the steam and hot water, as shown in **Figure 10.** The world's largest geothermal power plant in California, called *The Geysers,* produces electrical energy for 1.7 million households.

Geothermal energy can also be used to heat buildings. In this process, hot water and steam are used to heat a fluid. Then, this fluid is pumped through a building in order to heat the building. Buildings in Iceland are heated from the country's many geothermal sites in this way.

✓ Reading Check How do geothermal power plants obtain geothermal energy from the Earth?

Figure 10 **How a Geothermal Power Plant Works**

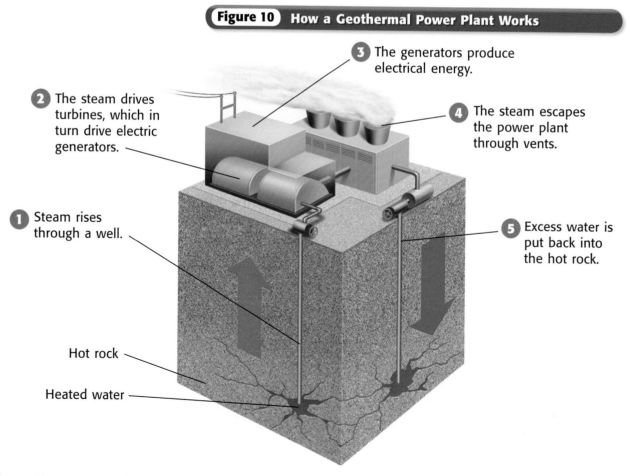

3 The generators produce electrical energy.

2 The steam drives turbines, which in turn drive electric generators.

4 The steam escapes the power plant through vents.

1 Steam rises through a well.

5 Excess water is put back into the hot rock.

Hot rock

Heated water

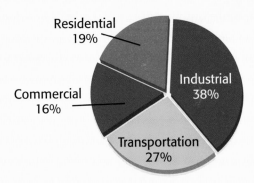

SECTION Review

Summary

- Fission and fusion are processes that release nuclear energy. The byproduct of fission is radioactive waste.

- For fusion to take place, extremely high temperatures are required.

- Fuel cells combine hydrogen and oxygen to produce electrical energy. Fuel cells release water as a byproduct.

- Solar energy is a renewable resource that doesn't emit pollution. However, solar panels and solar collectors are expensive.

- Wind power is a renewable resource that doesn't emit pollution. However, wind energy cannot be generated in all areas.

- Hydroelectric energy is a cheap, renewable resource that causes little pollution. However, it is available only in some areas.

- Burning biomass and gasohol can release energy, but not enough to meet all of our energy needs.

- Geothermal energy comes from the Earth but is available only in certain areas.

Using Key Terms

1. In your own words, write a definition for each of the following terms: *nuclear energy, solar energy, wind power, hydroelectric energy, biomass, gasohol,* and *geothermal energy.*

Understanding Key Ideas

2. Which of the following alternative resources requires hydrogen and oxygen to produce energy?
   a. fuel cells
   b. solar energy
   c. nuclear energy
   d. geothermal energy

3. Describe two ways of using solar energy.

4. Where is the production of hydroelectric energy practical?

5. Describe two ways to release biomass energy.

6. Describe two ways to use geothermal energy.

Critical Thinking

7. **Analyzing Methods** If you were going to build a nuclear power plant, why wouldn't you build it in the middle of a desert?

8. **Predicting Consequences** If an alternative resource could successfully replace crude oil, how might the use of that resource affect the environment?

Interpreting Graphics

Use the graph below to answer the questions that follow.

How Energy Is Used in the United States

Residential 19%

Industrial 38%

Commercial 16%

Transportation 27%

Source: International Energy Agency.

9. What is the total percentage of energy that is used for commercial and industrial purposes?

10. What is the total percentage of energy that is not used for residential purposes?

SciLINKS

NSTA

Developed and maintained by the National Science Teachers Association

For a variety of links related to this chapter, go to www.scilinks.org

Topic: Renewable Resources
SciLinks code: HSM1291

Model-Making Lab

Make a Water Wheel

Lift Enterprises is planning to build a water wheel that will lift objects like a crane does. The president of the company has asked you to modify the basic water wheel design so that the water wheel will lift objects more quickly.

OBJECTIVES

Create a model of a water wheel.

Determine factors that influence the rate at which a water wheel lifts a weight.

MATERIALS

- bottle, soda, 2 L, filled with water
- card, index, 3 × 5 in.
- clay, modeling
- coin
- cork
- glue
- hole punch
- jug, milk, plastic
- marker, permanent, black
- meterstick
- safety razor (for teacher)
- scissors
- skewers, wooden (2)
- tape, transparent
- thread, 20 cm
- thumbtacks (5)
- watch or clock that indicates seconds

SAFETY

Ask a Question

1 What factors influence the rate at which a water wheel lifts a weight?

Form a Hypothesis

2 Change the question above into a statement to formulate a testable hypothesis.

Test the Hypothesis

3 Build a water wheel model. Measure and mark a 5 × 5 cm square on an index card. Cut the square out of the card. Fold the square in half to form a triangle.

4 Measure and mark a line 8 cm from the bottom of the plastic jug. Use scissors to cut along this line. (Your teacher may need to use a safety razor to start this cut for you.)

5 Use the paper triangle you made in step 3 as a template. Use a permanent marker to trace four triangles onto the flat parts of the top section of the plastic jug. Cut the triangles out of the plastic to form four fins.

6 Use a thumbtack to attach one corner of each plastic fin to the round edge of the cork, as shown below. Make sure the fins are equally spaced around the cork.

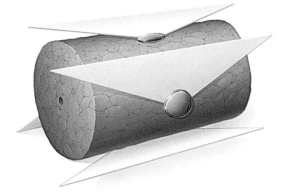

7 Press a thumbtack into one of the flat sides of the cork. Jiggle the thumbtack to widen the hole in the cork, and then remove the thumbtack. Repeat on the other side of the cork.

8 Place a drop of glue on one end of each skewer. Insert the first skewer into one of the holes in the end of the cork. Insert the second skewer into the hole in the other end of the cork.

9 Use a hole punch to carefully punch two holes in the bottom section of the plastic jug. Punch each hole 1 cm from the top edge of the jug, directly across from one another.

10 Carefully push the skewers through the holes, and suspend the cork in the center of the jug. Attach a small ball of clay to the end of each skewer. The balls should be the same size.

11 Tape one end of the thread to one skewer on the outside of the jug, next to the clay ball. Wrap the thread around the clay ball three times. (As the water wheel turns, the thread should wrap around the clay. The other ball of clay balances the weight and helps to keep the water wheel turning smoothly.)

12 Tape the free end of the thread to a coin. Wrap the thread around the coin, and tape it again.

13 Slowly pour water from the 2 L bottle onto the fins so that the water wheel spins. What happens to the coin? Record your observations.

14 Lower the coin back to the starting position. Add more clay to the skewer to increase the diameter of the wheel. Repeat step 13. Did the coin rise faster or slower this time?

15 Lower the coin back to the starting position. Modify the shape of the clay, and repeat step 13. Does the shape of the clay affect how quickly the coin rises? Explain your answer.

16 What happens if you remove two of the fins from opposite sides? What happens if you add more fins?

17 Experiment with another fin shape. How does a different fin shape affect how quickly the coin rises?

Analyze the Results

1 **Examining Data** What factors influence how quickly you can lift the coin? Explain.

Draw Conclusions

2 **Drawing Conclusions** What recommendations would you make to the president of Lift Enterprises to improve the water wheel?

Chapter Review

USING KEY TERMS

The statements below are false. For each statement, replace the underlined term to make a true statement.

1 A liquid mixture of complex hydrocarbon compounds is called <u>natural gas</u>.

2 Energy that is released when a chemical compound reacts to produce a new compound is called <u>nuclear energy</u>.

For each pair of terms, explain how the meanings of the terms differ.

3 *solar energy* and *wind power*

4 *biomass* and *gasohol*

UNDERSTANDING KEY IDEAS

Multiple Choice

5 Which of the following resources is a renewable resource?

a. coal   c. oil

b. trees   d. natural gas

6 Which of the following fuels is NOT made from petroleum?

a. jet fuel

b. lignite

c. kerosene

d. fuel oil

7 Peat, lignite, and anthracite are all forms of

a. petroleum.

b. natural gas.

c. coal.

d. gasohol.

8 Which of the following factors contributes to smog?

a. automobiles

b. sunlight

c. mountains surrounding urban areas

d. All of the above

9 Which of the following resources is produced by fusion?

a. solar energy

b. natural gas

c. nuclear energy

d. petroleum

10 To produce energy, nuclear power plants use a process called

a. fission.

b. fusion.

c. fractionation.

d. None of the above

11 A solar-powered calculator uses

a. solar collectors.

b. solar panels.

c. solar mirrors.

d. solar cells.

Short Answer

12 How does acid precipitation form?

13 If sunlight is free, why is electrical energy from solar cells expensive?

14 Describe three ways that humans use natural resources.

15 Explain how fossil fuels are found and obtained.

CRITICAL THINKING

16 Concept Mapping Use the following terms to create a concept map: *fossil fuels, wind energy, energy resources, biomass, renewable resources, solar energy, nonrenewable resources, natural gas, gasohol, coal,* and *oil*.

17 Predicting Consequences How would your life be different if fossil fuels were less widely available?

18 Evaluating Assumptions Are fossil fuels nonrenewable? Explain.

19 Evaluating Assumptions Why do we need to conserve renewable resources even though they can be replaced?

20 Evaluating Data What might limit the productivity of a geothermal power plant?

21 Identifying Relationships Explain why the energy we get from many of our resources ultimately comes from the sun.

22 Applying Concepts Describe the different ways you can conserve natural resources at home.

23 Identifying Relationships Explain why coal usually forms in different locations from where petroleum and natural gas form.

24 Applying Concepts Choose an alternative energy resource that you think should be developed more. Explain the reason for your choice.

INTERPRETING GRAPHICS

Use the graph below to answer the questions that follow.

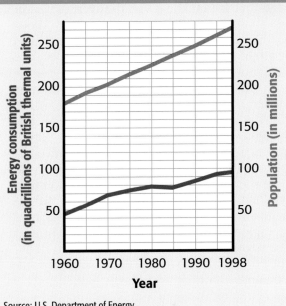

Energy Consumption and Population Growth in the United States

Source: U.S. Department of Energy.

25 How many British thermal units were consumed in 1970?

26 In what year was the most energy consumed?

27 Why do you think that energy consumption has not increased at the same rate as the population has increased?

Standardized Test Preparation

Read each of the passages below. Then, answer the questions that follow each passage.

Passage 1 Did you know that the average person creates about 2 kg of garbage every day? About 7% of this waste is <u>composed</u> of plastic products that can be recycled. Instead of adding to the landfill problem, you can recycle your plastic trash so that you can sit on it. Today, plastic is recycled into items such as park benches and highchairs. However, before plastic can be made into new products, it must be sorted. Plastic is sorted according to the resin codes that are printed on every recyclable plastic product. The resin code tells you the type of plastic that was used to make the product. The plastic most often recycled to make furniture includes the polyethylene plastic called high-density polyethylene, or HDPE, and low-density polyethylene, or LDPE. Both HDPE and LDPE are used to make items such as milk jugs, detergent bottles, and plastic bags.

1. In the passage, what does *composed* mean?
  A processed into
  B formed
  C crushed
  D melted

2. According to the passage, plastic products
  F can be recycled into highchairs.
  G can be recycled into cars.
  H cannot be recycled.
  I cause environmental problems.

3. According to the passage, which of the following statements is a fact?
  A The average person creates 7 kg of waste every day.
  B The average person weighs 7 kg.
  C LDPE can be used to make milk jugs, detergent bottles, plastic bags, and grocery bags.
  D Recycled plastics are too weak to be made into furniture.

Passage 2 You may have heard of the great California gold rush. In 1849, thousands of people moved west to California hoping to strike gold. But you may not have heard about another rush, which occurred 10 years later. What lured people to northwestern Pennsylvania in 1859? The thrill of striking oil did! However, people were using oil long before 1859. People started using oil as early as 3000 BCE. In Mesopotamia, oil was used to waterproof ships. The Egyptians and Chinese <u>utilized</u> oil as a medicine. It was not until the late 1700s and early 1800s that people began to use oil as a fuel for lamps to light homes and factories. Today, oil is most commonly used in transportation.

1. In the passage, what does *utilized* mean?
  A processed
  B drank
  C burned
  D used

2. According to the passage, which of the following statements is true?
  F Oil can be used to waterproof ships.
  G Oil wasn't discovered until 3000 BCE.
  H Oil was first used in Pennsylvania as a medicine.
  I Oil was used in transportation as early as 1849.

3. According to the passage, which of the following statements is a fact?
  A In 1849, people moved to Pennsylvania for a gold rush.
  B In 1649, people used oil to light homes and factories.
  C In 1849, people moved to California to find gold.
  D In 1849, people did not have any use for oil.

Below is a pie chart of how various energy resources meet the world's energy needs. Use this pie chart to answer the questions that follow.

Read each question below, and choose the best answer.

World Usage of Energy Resources

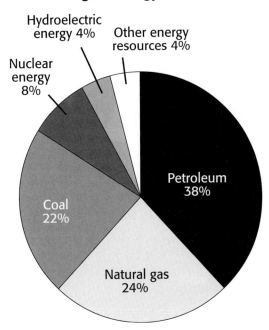

1. What percentage of the energy used in the world comes from coal?

   A 22%

   B 24%

   C 28%

   D 38%

2. What percentage of the energy used in the world comes from fossil fuels?

   F 54%

   G 84%

   H 96%

   I 100%

3. What is the total percentage of energy used for resources that do not include fossil fuels?

   A 3%

   B 16%

   C 24%

   D 64%

1. The ratio of the number of kilograms of aluminum recycled to the number of kilograms of newspaper recycled by a seventh-grade class is 34 to 170. What is this ratio written as a decimal?

   A 0.02

   B 0.2

   C 0.5

   D 5

2. Peat is about 60% carbon. Approximately how many kilograms of carbon would a 130 kg sample of peat contain?

   F 7.8 kg

   G 52 kg

   H 78 kg

   I 780 kg

3. If a 24 kg sample of anthracite is examined and 21.6 kg of carbon is found in the sample, what percentage of the sample is carbon?

   A 90%

   B 10%

   C 9%

   D 2.4%

4. Cora's car runs on alcohol made from corn. Cora drives her car 12,000 km per year, and her car's gas mileage is 30 km/L. If 200 L of alcohol can be obtained from each acre of corn that is processed, about how many acres of corn would Cora have to process to fuel her car for a year?

   F 1 acre

   G 2 acres

   H 8 acres

   I 50 acres

Standardized Test Preparation

Science in Action

Scientific Debate

The Three Gorges Dam

Dams provide hydroelectric energy, drinking water, and food for crops. Unfortunately, massive dam projects flood scenic landscapes and disrupt the environment around the dam. For example, the Three Gorges dam in China has displaced almost 2 million people living in the project area. Opponents of the project claim that the dam will also increase pollution levels in the Yangtze River. However, supporters of the dam say it will control flooding and provide millions of people with hydroelectric power. Engineers estimate that the dam's turbines will produce enough electrical energy to power a city 10 times the size of Los Angeles, California.

Science, Technology, and Society

Hybrid Cars

One solution to the pollution problem caused by the burning of fossil fuels for transportation purposes is to develop cars that depend less on fossil fuels. One such car is called a *hybrid*. Instead of using only gasoline for energy, a hybrid car uses gasoline and electricity. Because of its special batteries, the hybrid needs less gasoline to run than a car powered only by gasoline does. Some hybrids can have a gas mileage of as much as 45 mi/gal! Already, there are several models on the market to choose from. In the near future, you might see more hybrid cars on the roads.

Math ACTIVITY

Charlie's truck has a gas mileage of 17 mi/gal. Charlie drives his truck an average of 12,000 mi per year. Then, he sells the truck and buys a new hybrid car that has a gas mileage of 45 mi/gal. If gasoline costs $1.40 per gallon, how much money will Charlie save in a year by driving the hybrid car instead of his truck?

Language Arts ACTIVITY

WRITING SKILL Find out more about another dam project. Develop your own opinion on the project. What do you think the best outcome would be? Create a fictional story that expresses this outcome.

Fred Begay

Nuclear Physicist Generating energy by combining atoms is called *fusion*. This process is being developed by nuclear physicists, such as Dr. Fred Begay, at the Department of Energy's Los Alamos National Laboratory. Begay hopes to someday make fusion an alternative energy resource. Because fusion is the process that generates energy in the sun, Begay uses NASA satellites to study the sun. Begay explains that it is necessary to develop skills in abstract reasoning to study fusion. As a Navajo, Begay developed these skills while growing up at his Navajo home in Towaoc, Colorado, where his family taught him about nature. Today, Begay uses his skills not only to help develop a new energy resource but also to mentor Native American and minority students. In 1999, Begay won the Distinguished Scientist Award from the Society for Advancement of Chicanos and Native Americans in Science.

Social Studies ACTIVITY

Research the lifestyle of Native Americans before 1900. Then, create a poster that compares resources that Native Americans used before 1900 with resources that many people use today.

To learn more about these Science in Action topics, visit go.hrw.com and type in the keyword HZ5ENRF.

Current Science

Check out Current Science® articles related to this chapter by visiting go.hrw.com. Just type in the keyword HZ5CS05.

Model-Making Lab

Adaptation: It's a Way of Life

Since the beginning of life on Earth, species have had special characteristics called *adaptations* that have helped them survive changes in environmental conditions. Changes in a species' environment include climate changes, habitat destruction, or the extinction of prey. These things can cause a species to die out unless the species has a characteristic that helps it survive. For example, a species of bird may have an adaptation for eating sunflower seeds and ants. If the ant population dies out, the bird can still eat seeds and can therefore survive.

In this activity, you will explore several adaptations and design an organism with adaptations you choose. Then, you will describe how these adaptations help the organism survive.

MATERIALS

- arts-and-crafts materials, various
- markers, colored
- magazines for cutouts
- poster board
- scissors

SAFETY

Procedure

1. Study the chart below. Choose one adaptation from each column. For example, an organism might be a scavenger that burrows underground and has spikes on its tail!

Adaptations		
Diet	**Type of transportation**	**Special adaptation**
carnivore	flies	uses sensors to detect heat
herbivore	glides through the air	is active only at night and has excellent night vision
omnivore	burrows underground	changes colors to match its surroundings
scavenger	runs fast	has armor
decomposer	swims	has horns
	hops	can withstand extreme temperature changes
	walks	secretes a terrible and sickening scent
	climbs	has poison glands
	floats	has specialized front teeth
	slithers	has tail spikes
		stores oxygen in its cells so it does not have to breathe continuously
		one of your own invention

2 Design an organism that has the three adaptations you have chosen. Use poster board, colored markers, picture cutouts, or craft materials of your choosing to create your organism.

3 Write a caption on your poster describing your organism. Describe its appearance, its habitat, its niche, and the way its adaptations help it survive. Give your organism a two-part "scientific" name that is based on its characteristics.

4 Display your creation in your classroom. Share with classmates how you chose the adaptations for your organism.

Analyze the Results

1 What does your imaginary organism eat?

2 In what environment or habitat would your organism be most likely to survive—in the desert, tropical rain forest, plains, icecaps, mountains, or ocean? Explain your answer.

3 Is your creature a mammal, a reptile, an amphibian, a bird, or a fish? What modern organism (on Earth today) or ancient organism (extinct) is your imaginary organism most like? Explain the similarities between the two organisms. Do some research outside the lab, if necessary, to find out about a real organism that may be similar to your imaginary organism.

Draw Conclusions

4 If there were a sudden climate change, such as daily downpours of rain in a desert, would your imaginary organism survive? What adaptations for surviving such a change does it have?

Applying Your Data

Call or write to an agency such as the U.S. Fish and Wildlife Service to get a list of endangered species in your area. Choose an organism on that list. Describe the organism's niche and any special adaptations it has that help it survive. Find out why it is endangered and what is being done to protect it. Examine the illustration of the animal at right. Based on its physical characteristics, describe its habitat and niche. Is this a real animal?

Model-Making Lab

A Passel o' Pioneers

Succession is the natural process of the introduction and development of living things in an area. The area could be one that has never supported life before and has no soil, such as a recently cooled lava flow from a volcano. In an area where there is no soil, the process is called *primary succession.* In an area where soil already exists, such as an abandoned field or a forest after a fire, the process is called *secondary succession.*

In this investigation, you will build a model of secondary succession using natural soil.

Procedure

1 Place the natural soil you brought from home or the school-yard into the fishbowl, and dampen the soil with 250 mL of water. Cover the top of the fishbowl with plastic wrap, and place the fishbowl in a sunny window.
Caution: Do not touch your face, eyes, or mouth during this activity. Wash your hands thoroughly when you are finished.

2 For 2 weeks, observe the fishbowl for any new growth. Describe and draw any new organisms you observe. Record these and all other observations.

3 Identify and record the names of as many of these new organisms as you can.

MATERIALS

- balance
- graduated cylinder, 250 mL
- large fishbowl
- plastic wrap
- protective gloves
- soil from home or schoolyard, 500 g
- water, 250 mL

SAFETY

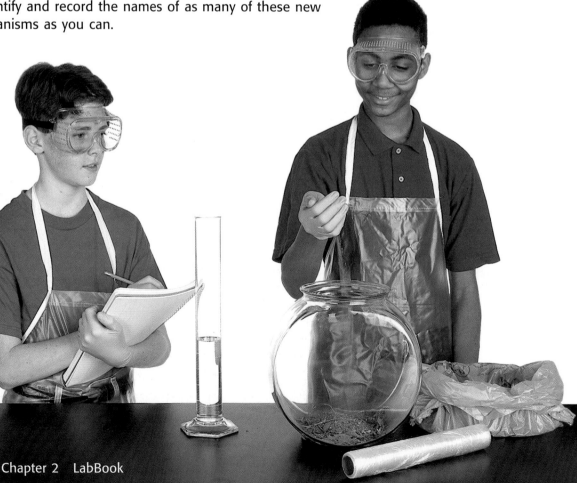

Analyze the Results

① What kinds of plants sprouted in your model of secondary succession? Were they tree seedlings, grasses, or weeds?

② Were the plants that sprouted in the fishbowl unusual or common for your area?

Draw Conclusions

③ Explain how the plants that grew in your model of secondary succession can be called pioneer species.

Applying Your Data

Examine each of the photographs on this page. Determine whether each area, if abandoned forever, would undergo primary or secondary succession. You may decide that an area will not undergo succession at all. Explain your reasoning.

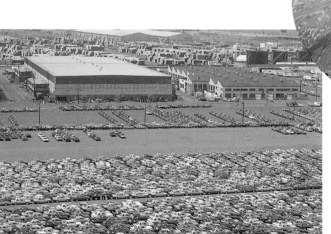

Bulldozed land

Eutrophic pond

Mount St. Helens volcano

Shipping port parking lot

Inquiry Lab

Life in the Desert

MATERIALS

- balance
- sponge, dry, 8 cm × 8 cm × 2 cm (2 pieces)
- water
- other materials as needed

Organisms that live in the desert have some unusual methods for conserving water. Conserving water is a special challenge for animals that live in the desert. In this activity you will invent a water-conserving "adaptation" for a desert animal, represented by a piece of sponge. You will protect your wet desert sponge so it will dry out as little as possible over a 24 h period.

Ask a Question

1 How can an animal conserve water in the desert?

Form a Hypothesis

2 Plan a method for keeping your "desert animal" from drying out. Your "animal" must be in the open for at least 4 h during the 24 h period. Real desert animals expose themselves to the dry desert heat to search for food. Write your plan and predictions about the outcome of your experiment.

3 Design and draw data tables, if necessary. Have your teacher approve your plan before you begin.

Test the Hypothesis

4 Soak two pieces of sponge in water until they begin to drip. Place each piece on a balance, and record its mass.

5 Immediately protect one sponge according to your plan. Place both pieces in an area where they will not be disturbed. You should take your protected "animal" out for feeding for a total of at least 4 h.

6 At the end of 24 h, place each piece of sponge on the balance again, and record its mass.

Analyze the Results

1 Describe the adaptation you used to help your "animal" survive. Was it effective? Explain.

2 What was the purpose of leaving one of the sponges unprotected? How did the water loss in each of your sponges compare?

Communicating Your Data

Conduct a class discussion about other adaptations and results. How can you relate these invented adaptations to adaptations for desert survival among real organisms?

Inquiry Lab

Discovering Mini-Ecosystems

In your study of ecosystems, you learned that a biome is a very large ecosystem that includes a set of smaller, related ecosystems. For example, a coniferous forest biome may include a river ecosystem, a wetland ecosystem, and a lake ecosystem. Each of those ecosystems may include several other smaller, related ecosystems. Even cities have mini-ecosystems! You may find a mini-ecosystem on a patch of sidewalk, in a puddle of rainwater, under a leaky faucet, in a shady area, or under a rock. In this activity, you will design a method for comparing two different mini-ecosystems found near your school.

MATERIALS

- items to be determined by the students and approved by the teacher

SAFETY

Ask a Question

1. Examine the grounds around your school, and select two different areas you wish to investigate. Decide what you want to learn about your mini-ecosystems. For example, you may want to know what kind of living things each area contains. Be sure to get your teacher's approval before you begin.

Form a Hypothesis

2. For each mini-ecosystem, make data tables for recording your observations.

Test the Hypothesis

3. Observe your mini-ecosystem according to your plan at several different time points throughout the day. Record your observations.

4. Wait 24 h and observe your mini-ecosystem again at the same times that you observed it the day before. Record your observations.

5. Wait 1 week, and observe your mini-ecosystem again at the same times. Record your observations.

Analyze the Results

1. What factors determine the differences between your mini-ecosystems? Identify the factors that set each mini-ecosystem apart from its surrounding area.

2. How do the populations of your mini-ecosystems compare?

3. Identify some of the adaptations that the organisms living in your two mini-ecosystems have. Describe how the adaptations help the organisms survive in their environment.

Draw Conclusions

4. Write a report describing and comparing your mini-ecosystems with those of your classmates.

Skills Practice Lab

Power of the Sun

The sun radiates energy in every direction. Like the sun, the energy radiated by a light bulb spreads out in all directions. But how much energy an object receives depends on how close that object is to the source. As you move farther from the source, the amount of energy you receive decreases. For example, if you measure the amount of energy that reaches you from a light and then move three times farther away, you will discover that nine times less energy will reach you at your second position. Energy from the sun travels as light energy. When light energy is absorbed by an object it is converted into thermal energy. Power is the rate at which one form of energy is converted to another, and it is measured in watts. Because power is related to distance, nearby objects can be used to measure the power of far-away objects. In this lab you will calculate the power of the sun using an ordinary 100-watt light bulb.

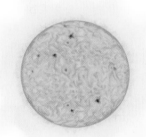

MATERIALS

- aluminum strip, 2 × 8 cm
- calculator, scientific
- clay, modeling
- desk lamp with a 100 W bulb and removable shade
- gloves, protective
- marker, black permanent
- mason jar, cap, and lid with hole in center
- pencil
- ruler, metric
- thermometer, Celsius
- watch (or clock) that indicates seconds

SAFETY

Procedure

1. Gently shape the piece of aluminum around a pencil so that it holds on in the middle and has two wings, one on either side of the pencil.

2. Bend the wings outward so that they can catch as much sunlight as possible.

3. Use the marker to color both wings on one side of the aluminum strip black.

4. Remove the pencil and place the aluminum snugly around the thermometer near the bulb. **Caution:** Do not press too hard—you do not want to break the thermometer! Wear protective gloves when working with the thermometer and the aluminum.

5. Carefully slide the top of the thermometer through the hole in the lid. Place the lid on the jar so that the thermometer bulb is inside the jar, and screw down the cap.

6. Secure the thermometer to the jar lid by molding clay around the thermometer on the outside of the lid. The aluminum wings should be in the center of the jar.

7. Read the temperature on the thermometer. Record this as room temperature.

8. Place the jar on a windowsill in the sunlight. Turn the jar so that the black wings are angled toward the sun.

9. Watch the thermometer until the temperature reading stops rising. Record the temperature.

10. Remove the jar from direct sunlight, and allow it to return to room temperature.

11. Remove any shade or reflector from the lamp. Place the lamp at one end of a table.

12. Place the jar about 30 cm from the lamp. Turn the jar so that the wings are angled toward the lamp.

13 Turn on the lamp, and wait about 1 minute.

14 Move the jar a few centimeters toward the lamp until the temperature reading starts to rise. When the temperature stops rising, compare it with the reading you took in step 9.

15 Repeat step 14 until the temperature matches the temperature you recorded in step 9.

16 If the temperature reading rises too high, move the jar away from the lamp and allow it to cool. Once the reading has dropped to at least 5°C below the temperature you recorded in step 9, you may begin again at step 12.

17 When the temperature in the jar matches the temperature you recorded in step 9, record the distance between the center of the light bulb and the thermometer bulb.

Analyze the Results

1 The thermometer measured the same amount of energy absorbed by the jar at the distance you measured to the lamp. In other words, your jar absorbed as much energy from the sun at a distance of 150 million kilometers as it did from the 100 W light bulb at the distance you recorded in step 17.

2 Use the following formula to calculate the power of the sun (be sure to show your work):

$$\frac{\text{power of the sun}}{(\text{distance to the sun})^2} = \frac{\text{power of the lamp}}{(\text{distance to the lamp})^2}$$

Hint: $(\text{distance})^2$ means that you multiply the distance by itself. If you found that the lamp was 5 cm away from the jar, for example, the $(\text{distance})^2$ would be 25.

Hint: Convert 150,000,000 km to 15,000,000,000,000 cm.

3 Review the discussion of scientific notation in the Math Refresher found in the Appendix at the back of this book. You will need to understand this technique for writing large numbers in order to compare your calculation with the actual figure. For practice, convert the distance to the sun given above in step 2 of Analyze the Results to scientific notation.

$$15,000,000,000,000 \text{ cm} = 1.5 \times 10^{\underline{?}} \text{ cm}$$

Draw Conclusions

4 The sun emits 3.7×10^{26} W of power. Compare your answer in step 2 with this value. Was this a good way to calculate the power of the sun? Explain.

✓ *Reading Check* Answers

Chapter 1   Interactions of Living Things

Section 1
Page 7:   The biosphere is the part of Earth where life exists.

Section 2
Page 9:   Organisms that eat other organisms are called *consumers*.

Page 11:   An energy pyramid is a diagram that shows an ecosystem's loss of energy.

Page 12:   Other animals in Yellowstone National Park were affected by the disappearance of the gray wolf because the food web was interrupted. The animals that would normally be prey for the gray wolf were more plentiful. These larger populations ate more vegetation.

Section 3
Page 15:   The main ways that organisms affect each other are through competition, predator and prey relationships, symbiotic relationships, and coevolution.

Page 17:   Camouflage helps an organism blend in with its surroundings because of its coloring. It is harder for a predator to find a camouflaged prey.

Page 20:   In a mutualistic relationship, both organisms benefit from the relationship.

Page 22:   Flowers need to attract pollinators to help the flowers reproduce with other members of their species.

Chapter 2   Cycles in Nature

Section 1
Page 33:   Without water, there would be no life on Earth.

Page 35:   Sample answer: calcium

Section 2
Page 36:   Plants grew back, and the area is recovering.

Page 38:   Primary succession happens in an area where organisms did not previously exist; secondary succession happens where organisms already exist.

Chapter 3   The Earth's Ecosystems

Section 1
Page 51:   Sample answer: *Deciduous* comes from a Latin word that means "to fall off." In temperate deciduous forests, the trees lose their leaves in the fall.

Page 52:   evergreen trees; squirrels, insects, finches, chickadees, jays, porcupines, elk, and moose

Page 54:   During the dry season, grasses on the savanna dry out and turn yellow. But their deep roots survive for many months without water.

Page 55:   Sample answer: Desert plants grow far apart. Some plants have shallow, widespread roots to take up water after a storm. Some desert plants have fleshy stems and leaves to store water. They also have waxy coatings to prevent water loss.

Page 56:   Sample answer: Alpine tundra is tundra found at the top of tall mountains, above the tree line.

Section 2
Page 58:   Sample answer: Plankton are tiny organisms that float near the surface of the water. They form the base of the ocean's feeding relationships.

Page 59:   Sample answer: Fishes that live near the poles have adaptations for the near-freezing water. Animals in coral reefs need warm water to live. Some animals migrate to warmer waters to reproduce. Water temperature affects whether some animals can eat.

Page 61:   Sample answer: Some animals get food from material that sinks to the bottom from the surface. Other animals get energy from chemicals released by thermal vents.

Page 62:   Sample answer: When corals die, they leave behind their skeletons. Other corals grow on these remains. Over time, the layers build up to form a coral reef.

Section 3
Page 65:   Sample answer: The littoral zone is the zone closest to shore in which light reaches the lake bottom. The open zone extends from the littoral zone and goes as deep as sunlight can reach. The deep-water zone lies beneath the open-water zone.

Page 66:   A swamp is a wetland ecosystem in which trees and vines grow.

Page 67:   Sample answer: Many fishes will die as the pond fills in because bacteria that decompose material in the pond use up the oxygen in the water.

Chapter 4 Environmental Problems and Solutions

Section 1

Page 78: Sample answer: Hazardous waste is waste that can catch fire, wear through metal, explode, or make people sick.

Page 81: Sample answer: Exotic species are organisms that make a home for themselves in a new place.

Page 82: Point-source pollution is pollution that comes from one place. Nonpoint-source pollution is pollution that comes from many places.

Section 2

Page 84: reduce, reuse, and recycle

Page 86: Sample answer: Water is reclaimed with plants or filter-feeding animals. Then, it can be used to water crops, parks, lawns, and golf courses.

Page 89: Sample answer: The EPA is a government organization that helps protect the environment.

Chapter 5 Energy Resources

Section 1

Page 103: A renewable resource is a natural resource that can be replaced at the same rate at which the resource is used.

Page 105: Answers may vary. Sample answer: newspapers, plastic containers, and cardboard boxes.

Section 2

Page 107: Natural gas is most often used for heating and for generating electrical energy.

Page 108: Coal was most commonly used to power trains.

Page 111: Natural gas and petroleum are removed from the Earth by drilling wells into rock that contains petroleum and natural gas.

Page 112: The sulfur dioxide released from the burning coal combines with moisture in the air to produce acid rain.

Section 3

Page 115: Fusion produces few dangerous wastes.

Page 116: The energy of fossil fuels comes from the sun.

Page 118: Hydroelectric energy is renewable because water is constantly recycled.

Page 120: Geothermal power plants obtain energy from the Earth by pumping steam and hot water from wells drilled into the rock.

Study Skills

FoldNote Instructions

Have you ever tried to study for a test or quiz but didn't know where to start? Or have you read a chapter and found that you can remember only a few ideas? Well, FoldNotes are a fun and exciting way to help you learn and remember the ideas you encounter as you learn science!

FoldNotes are tools that you can use to organize concepts. By focusing on a few main concepts, FoldNotes help you learn and remember how the concepts fit together. They can help you see the "big picture." Below you will find instructions for building 10 different FoldNotes.

Pyramid

1. Place a sheet of paper in front of you. Fold the lower left-hand corner of the paper diagonally to the opposite edge of the paper.

2. Cut off the tab of paper created by the fold (at the top).

3. Open the paper so that it is a square. Fold the lower right-hand corner of the paper diagonally to the opposite corner to form a triangle.

4. Open the paper. The creases of the two folds will have created an X.

5. Using scissors, cut along one of the creases. Start from any corner, and stop at the center point to create two flaps. Use tape or glue to attach one of the flaps on top of the other flap.

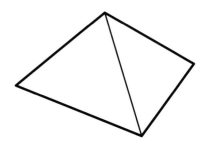

Double Door

1. Fold a sheet of paper in half from the top to the bottom. Then, unfold the paper.

2. Fold the top and bottom edges of the paper to the crease.

Booklet

1. Fold a sheet of paper in half from left to right. Then, unfold the paper.

2. Fold the sheet of paper in half again from the top to the bottom. Then, unfold the paper.

3. Refold the sheet of paper in half from left to right.

4. Fold the top and bottom edges to the center crease.

5. Completely unfold the paper.

6. Refold the paper from top to bottom.

7. Using scissors, cut a slit along the center crease of the sheet from the folded edge to the creases made in step 4. Do not cut the entire sheet in half.

8. Fold the sheet of paper in half from left to right. While holding the bottom and top edges of the paper, push the bottom and top edges together so that the center collapses at the center slit. Fold the four flaps to form a four-page book.

Layered Book

1. Lay one sheet of paper on top of another sheet. Slide the top sheet up so that 2 cm of the bottom sheet is showing.

2. Hold the two sheets together, fold down the top of the two sheets so that you see four 2 cm tabs along the bottom.

3. Using a stapler, staple the top of the FoldNote.

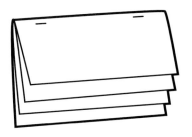

Key-Term Fold

1. Fold a sheet of lined notebook paper in half from left to right.

2. Using scissors, cut along every third line from the right edge of the paper to the center fold to make tabs.

Four-Corner Fold

1. Fold a sheet of paper in half from left to right. Then, unfold the paper.

2. Fold each side of the paper to the crease in the center of the paper.

3. Fold the paper in half from the top to the bottom. Then, unfold the paper.

4. Using scissors, cut the top flap creases made in step 3 to form four flaps.

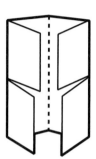

Three-Panel Flip Chart

1. Fold a piece of paper in half from the top to the bottom.

2. Fold the paper in thirds from side to side. Then, unfold the paper so that you can see the three sections.

3. From the top of the paper, cut along each of the vertical fold lines to the fold in the middle of the paper. You will now have three flaps.

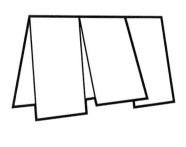

Table Fold

1. Fold a piece of paper in half from the top to the bottom. Then, fold the paper in half again.

2. Fold the paper in thirds from side to side.

3. Unfold the paper completely. Carefully trace the fold lines by using a pen or pencil.

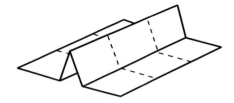

Two-Panel Flip Chart

1. Fold a piece of paper in half from the top to the bottom.

2. Fold the paper in half from side to side. Then, unfold the paper so that you can see the two sections.

3. From the top of the paper, cut along the vertical fold line to the fold in the middle of the paper. You will now have two flaps.

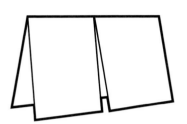

Tri-Fold

1. Fold a piece a paper in thirds from the top to the bottom.

2. Unfold the paper so that you can see the three sections. Then, turn the paper sideways so that the three sections form vertical columns.

3. Trace the fold lines by using a pen or pencil. Label the columns "Know," "Want," and "Learn."

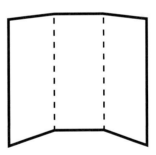

Graphic Organizer Instructions

Have you ever wished that you could "draw out" the many concepts you learn in your science class? Sometimes, being able to *see* how concepts are related really helps you remember what you've learned. Graphic Organizers do just that! They give you a way to draw or map out concepts.

All you need to make a Graphic Organizer is a piece of paper and a pencil. Below you will find instructions for four different Graphic Organizers designed to help you organize the concepts you'll learn in this book.

Spider Map

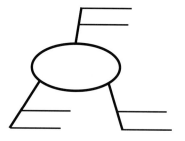

1. Draw a diagram like the one shown. In the circle, write the main topic.

2. From the circle, draw legs to represent different categories of the main topic. You can have as many categories as you want.

3. From the category legs, draw horizontal lines. As you read the chapter, write details about each category on the horizontal lines.

Comparison Table

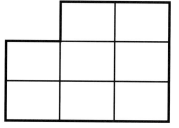

1. Draw a chart like the one shown. Your chart can have as many columns and rows as you want.

2. In the top row, write the topics that you want to compare.

3. In the left column, write characteristics of the topics that you want to compare. As you read the chapter, fill in the characteristics for each topic in the appropriate boxes.

Appendix

Chain-of-Events-Chart

1. Draw a box. In the box, write the first step of a process or the first event of a timeline.

2. Under the box, draw another box, and use an arrow to connect the two boxes. In the second box, write the next step of the process or the next event in the timeline.

3. Continue adding boxes until the process or timeline is finished.

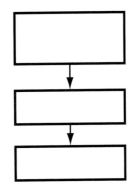

Concept Map

1. Draw a circle in the center of a piece of paper. Write the main idea of the chapter in the center of the circle.

2. From the circle, draw other circles. In those circles, write characteristics of the main idea. Draw arrows from the center circle to the circles that contain the characteristics.

3. From each circle that contains a characteristic, draw other circles. In those circles, write specific details about the characteristic. Draw arrows from each circle that contains a characteristic to the circles that contain specific details. You may draw as many circles as you want.

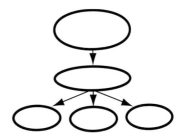

Scientific Methods

The ways in which scientists answer questions and solve problems are called **scientific methods.** The same steps are often used by scientists as they look for answers. However, there is more than one way to use these steps. Scientists may use all of the steps or just some of the steps during an investigation. They may even repeat some of the steps. The goal of using scientific methods is to come up with reliable answers and solutions.

Six Steps of Scientific Methods

Ask a Question

Good questions come from careful **observations.** You make observations by using your senses to gather information. Sometimes, you may use instruments, such as microscopes and telescopes, to extend the range of your senses. As you observe the natural world, you will discover that you have many more questions than answers. These questions drive investigations.

Questions beginning with *what, why, how,* and *when* are important in focusing an investigation. Here is an example of a question that could lead to an investigation.

Question: How does acid rain affect plant growth?

Form a Hypothesis

After you ask a question, you need to form a **hypothesis.** A hypothesis is a clear statement of what you expect the answer to your question to be. Your hypothesis will represent your best "educated guess" based on what you have observed and what you already know. A good hypothesis is testable. Otherwise, the investigation can go no further. Here is a hypothesis based on the question, "How does acid rain affect plant growth?"

Hypothesis: Acid rain slows plant growth.

The hypothesis can lead to predictions. A prediction is what you think the outcome of your experiment or data collection will be. Predictions are usually stated in an if-then format. Here is a sample prediction for the hypothesis that acid rain slows plant growth.

Prediction: If a plant is watered with only acid rain (which has a pH of 4), then the plant will grow at half its normal rate.

Test the Hypothesis

After you have formed a hypothesis and made a prediction, your hypothesis should be tested. One way to test a hypothesis is with a controlled experiment. A **controlled experiment** tests only one factor at a time. In an experiment to test the effect of acid rain on plant growth, the **control group** would be watered with normal rain water. The **experimental group** would be watered with acid rain. All of the plants should receive the same amount of sunlight and water each day. The air temperature should be the same for all groups. However, the acidity of the water will be a variable. In fact, any factor that is different from one group to another is a **variable.** If your hypothesis is correct, then the acidity of the water and plant growth are *dependant variables.* The amount a plant grows is dependent on the acidity of the water. However, the amount of water each plant receives and the amount of sunlight each plant receives are *independent variables.* Either of these factors could change without affecting the other factor.

Sometimes, the nature of an investigation makes a controlled experiment impossible. For example, the Earth's core is surrounded by thousands of meters of rock. Under such circumstances, a hypothesis may be tested by making detailed observations.

Analyze the Results

After you have completed your experiments, made your observations, and collected your data, you must analyze all the information you have gathered. Tables and graphs are often used in this step to organize the data.

5 Draw Conclusions

After analyzing your data, you can determine if your results support your hypothesis. If your hypothesis is supported, you (or others) might want to repeat the observations or experiments to verify your results. If your hypothesis is not supported by the data, you may have to check your procedure for errors. You may even have to reject your hypothesis and make a new one. If you cannot draw a conclusion from your results, you may have to try the investigation again or carry out further observations or experiments.

6 Communicate Results

After any scientific investigation, you should report your results. By preparing a written or oral report, you let others know what you have learned. They may repeat your investigation to see if they get the same results. Your report may even lead to another question and then to another investigation.

Scientific Methods in Action

Scientific methods contain loops in which several steps may be repeated over and over again. In some cases, certain steps are unnecessary. Thus, there is not a "straight line" of steps. For example, sometimes scientists find that testing one hypothesis raises new questions and new hypotheses to be tested. And sometimes, testing the hypothesis leads directly to a conclusion. Furthermore, the steps in scientific methods are not always used in the same order. Follow the steps in the diagram, and see how many different directions scientific methods can take you.

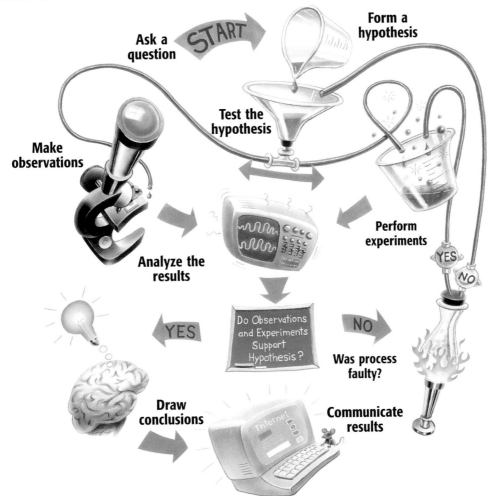

Math Refresher

Science requires an understanding of many math concepts. The following pages will help you review some important math skills.

Averages

An **average**, or **mean**, simplifies a set of numbers into a single number that *approximates* the value of the set.

> **Example:** Find the average of the following set of numbers: 5, 4, 7, and 8.

Step 1: Find the sum.
$$5 + 4 + 7 + 8 = 24$$

Step 2: Divide the sum by the number of numbers in your set. Because there are four numbers in this example, divide the sum by 4.
$$\frac{24}{4} = 6$$

The average, or mean, is **6.**

Ratios

A **ratio** is a comparison between numbers, and it is usually written as a fraction.

> **Example:** Find the ratio of thermometers to students if you have 36 thermometers and 48 students in your class.

Step 1: Make the ratio.
$$\frac{36 \text{ thermometers}}{48 \text{ students}}$$

Step 2: Reduce the fraction to its simplest form.
$$\frac{36}{48} = \frac{36 \div 12}{48 \div 12} = \frac{3}{4}$$

The ratio of thermometers to students is **3 to 4,** or $\frac{3}{4}$. The ratio may also be written in the form 3:4.

Proportions

A **proportion** is an equation that states that two ratios are equal.
$$\frac{3}{1} = \frac{12}{4}$$

To solve a proportion, first multiply across the equal sign. This is called *cross-multiplication*. If you know three of the quantities in a proportion, you can use cross-multiplication to find the fourth.

> **Example:** Imagine that you are making a scale model of the solar system for your science project. The diameter of Jupiter is 11.2 times the diameter of the Earth. If you are using a plastic-foam ball that has a diameter of 2 cm to represent the Earth, what must the diameter of the ball representing Jupiter be?
> $$\frac{11.2}{1} = \frac{x}{2 \text{ cm}}$$

Step 1: Cross-multiply.
$$\frac{11.2}{1} \diagdown\!\!\!\!\diagup \frac{x}{2}$$
$$11.2 \times 2 = x \times 1$$

Step 2: Multiply.
$$22.4 = x \times 1$$

Step 3: Isolate the variable by dividing both sides by 1.
$$x = \frac{22.4}{1}$$
$$x = 22.4 \text{ cm}$$

You will need to use a ball that has a diameter of **22.4** cm to represent Jupiter.

Percentages

A **percentage** is a ratio of a given number to 100.

> **Example:** What is 85% of 40?

Step 1: Rewrite the percentage by moving the decimal point two places to the left.

$$0.85$$

Step 2: Multiply the decimal by the number that you are calculating the percentage of.

$$0.85 \times 40 = 34$$

85% of 40 is **34.**

Decimals

To **add** or **subtract decimals,** line up the digits vertically so that the decimal points line up. Then, add or subtract the columns from right to left. Carry or borrow numbers as necessary.

> **Example:** Add the following numbers: 3.1415 and 2.96.

Step 1: Line up the digits vertically so that the decimal points line up.

$$\begin{array}{r} 3.1415 \\ + 2.96 \\ \hline \end{array}$$

Step 2: Add the columns from right to left, and carry when necessary.

$$\begin{array}{r} {}^{1\ 1} \\ 3.1415 \\ + 2.96 \\ \hline 6.1015 \end{array}$$

The sum is **6.1015.**

Fractions

Numbers tell you how many; **fractions** tell you *how much of a whole*.

> **Example:** Your class has 24 plants. Your teacher instructs you to put 5 plants in a shady spot. What fraction of the plants in your class will you put in a shady spot?

Step 1: In the denominator, write the total number of parts in the whole.

$$\frac{?}{24}$$

Step 2: In the numerator, write the number of parts of the whole that are being considered.

$$\frac{5}{24}$$

So, $\frac{5}{24}$ of the plants will be in the shade.

Reducing Fractions

It is usually best to express a fraction in its simplest form. Expressing a fraction in its simplest form is called *reducing* a fraction.

> **Example:** Reduce the fraction $\frac{30}{45}$ to its simplest form.

Step 1: Find the largest whole number that will divide evenly into both the numerator and denominator. This number is called the *greatest common factor* (GCF).

Factors of the numerator 30:
1, 2, 3, 5, 6, 10, **15,** 30

Factors of the denominator 45:
1, 3, 5, 9, **15,** 45

Step 2: Divide both the numerator and the denominator by the GCF, which in this case is 15.

$$\frac{30}{45} = \frac{30 \div 15}{45 \div 15} = \frac{2}{3}$$

Thus, $\frac{30}{45}$ reduced to its simplest form is $\frac{2}{3}$.

Adding and Subtracting Fractions

To **add** or **subtract fractions** that have the **same denominator,** simply add or subtract the numerators.

Examples:

$$\frac{3}{5} + \frac{1}{5} = ? \text{ and } \frac{3}{4} - \frac{1}{4} = ?$$

Step 1: Add or subtract the numerators.

$$\frac{3}{5} + \frac{1}{5} = \frac{4}{} \text{ and } \frac{3}{4} - \frac{1}{4} = \frac{2}{}$$

Step 2: Write the sum or difference over the denominator.

$$\frac{3}{5} + \frac{1}{5} = \frac{4}{5} \text{ and } \frac{3}{4} - \frac{1}{4} = \frac{2}{4}$$

Step 3: If necessary, reduce the fraction to its simplest form.

$\frac{4}{5}$ cannot be reduced, and $\frac{2}{4} = \frac{1}{2}$.

To **add** or **subtract fractions** that have **different denominators,** first find the least common denominator (LCD).

Examples:

$$\frac{1}{2} + \frac{1}{6} = ? \text{ and } \frac{3}{4} - \frac{2}{3} = ?$$

Step 1: Write the equivalent fractions that have a common denominator.

$$\frac{3}{6} + \frac{1}{6} = ? \text{ and } \frac{9}{12} - \frac{8}{12} = ?$$

Step 2: Add or subtract the fractions.

$$\frac{3}{6} + \frac{1}{6} = \frac{4}{6} \text{ and } \frac{9}{12} - \frac{8}{12} = \frac{1}{12}$$

Step 3: If necessary, reduce the fraction to its simplest form.

The fraction $\frac{4}{6} = \frac{2}{3}$, and $\frac{1}{12}$ cannot be reduced.

Multiplying Fractions

To **multiply fractions,** multiply the numerators and the denominators together, and then reduce the fraction to its simplest form.

Example:

$$\frac{5}{9} \times \frac{7}{10} = ?$$

Step 1: Multiply the numerators and denominators.

$$\frac{5}{9} \times \frac{7}{10} = \frac{5 \times 7}{9 \times 10} = \frac{35}{90}$$

Step 2: Reduce the fraction.

$$\frac{35}{90} = \frac{35 \div 5}{90 \div 5} = \frac{7}{18}$$

Dividing Fractions

To **divide fractions,** first rewrite the divisor (the number you divide by) upside down. This number is called the *reciprocal* of the divisor. Then multiply and reduce if necessary.

Example:

$$\frac{5}{8} \div \frac{3}{2} = ?$$

Step 1: Rewrite the divisor as its reciprocal.

$$\frac{3}{2} \rightarrow \frac{2}{3}$$

Step 2: Multiply the fractions.

$$\frac{5}{8} \times \frac{2}{3} = \frac{5 \times 2}{8 \times 3} = \frac{10}{24}$$

Step 3: Reduce the fraction.

$$\frac{10}{24} = \frac{10 \div 2}{24 \div 2} = \frac{5}{12}$$

Scientific Notation

Scientific notation is a short way of representing very large and very small numbers without writing all of the place-holding zeros.

Example: Write 653,000,000 in scientific notation.

Step 1: Write the number without the place-holding zeros.

653

Step 2: Place the decimal point after the first digit.

6.53

Step 3: Find the exponent by counting the number of places that you moved the decimal point.

6.53000000

The decimal point was moved eight places to the left. Therefore, the exponent of 10 is positive 8. If you had moved the decimal point to the right, the exponent would be negative.

Step 4: Write the number in scientific notation.

6.53×10^8

Area

Area is the number of square units needed to cover the surface of an object.

Formulas:

area of a square = side × side
area of a rectangle = length × width
area of a triangle = $\frac{1}{2}$ × base × height

Examples: Find the areas.

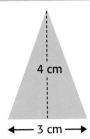

Triangle

area = $\frac{1}{2}$ × base × height
area = $\frac{1}{2}$ × 3 cm × 4 cm
*area = **6 cm²***

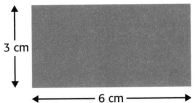

Rectangle
area = length × width
area = 6 cm × 3 cm
*area = **18 cm²***

Square
area = side × side
area = 3 cm × 3 cm
*area = **9 cm²***

Volume

Volume is the amount of space that something occupies.

Formulas:

volume of a cube =
side × side × side

volume of a prism =
area of base × height

Examples:

Find the volume of the solids.

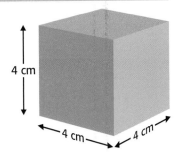

Cube
volume = side × side × side
volume = 4 cm × 4 cm × 4 cm
*volume = **64 cm³***

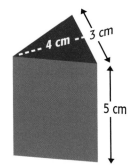

Prism
volume = area of base × height
volume = (area of triangle) × height
volume = ($\frac{1}{2}$ × 3 cm × 4 cm) × 5 cm
volume = 6 cm² × 5 cm
*volume = **30 cm³***

Appendix

Glossary

A

abiotic describes the nonliving part of the environment, including water, rocks, light, and temperature (4)

acid precipitation rain, sleet, or snow that contains a high concentration of acids (112)

B

biodiversity the number and variety of organisms in a given area during a specific period of time (82)

biomass organic matter that can be a source of energy; the total mass of the organisms in a given area (119)

biome (BIE OHM) a large region characterized by a specific type of climate and certain types of plant and animal communities (50)

biosphere the part of Earth where life exists (7)

biotic describes living factors in the environment (4)

C

carnivore an organism that eats animals (9)

carrying capacity the largest population that an environment can support at any given time (15)

chemical energy the energy released when a chemical compound reacts to produce new compounds (116)

coal a fossil fuel that forms underground from partially decomposed plant material (108)

coevolution the evolution of two species that is due to mutual influence, often in a way that makes the relationship more beneficial to both species (19)

combustion the burning of a substance (34)

commensalism a relationship between two organisms in which one organism benefits and the other is unaffected (18)

community all of the populations of species that live in the same habitat and interact with each other (6)

condensation the change of state from a gas to a liquid (32)

conservation (KAHN suhr VAY shuhn) the preservation and wise use of natural resources (84)

consumer an organism that eats other organisms or organic matter

D

decomposer an organism that gets energy by breaking down the remains of dead organisms or animal wastes and consuming or absorbing the nutrients

decomposition the breakdown of substances into simpler molecular substances (34)

deep-water zone the zone of a lake or pond below the open-water zone, where no light reaches (65)

desert an area that has little or no plant life, long periods without rain, and extreme temperatures; usually found in hot climates (55)

E

ecology the study of the interactions of living organisms with one another and with their environment (4)

ecosystem a community of organisms and their abiotic, or nonliving, environment (7)

energy pyramid a triangular diagram that shows an ecosystem's loss of energy, which results as energy passes through the ecosystem's food chain (11)

estuary (ES tyoo er ee) an area where fresh water from rivers mixes with salt water from the ocean (62)

evaporation the change of a substance from a liquid to a gas (32)

F

food chain the pathway of energy transfer through various stages as a result of the feeding patterns of a series of organisms (10)

food web a diagram that shows the feeding relationships between organisms in an ecosystem (10)

fossil fuel a nonrenewable energy resource formed from the remains of organisms that lived long ago (106)

G

gasohol a mixture of gasoline and alcohol that is used as a fuel (119)

geothermal energy the energy produced by heat within the Earth (120)

H

herbivore an organism that eats only plants (9)

host an organism from which a parasite takes food or shelter

hydroelectric energy electrical energy produced by falling water (118)

L

littoral zone (LIT uh ruhl ZOHN) the shallow zone of a lake or pond where light reaches the bottom and nurtures plants (65)

M

marsh a treeless wetland ecosystem where plants such as grasses grow (66)

mutualism (MYOO choo uhl IZ uhm) a relationship between two species in which both species benefit (18)

N

natural gas a mixture of gaseous hydrocarbons located under the surface of the Earth, often near petroleum deposits; used as a fuel (107)

natural resource any natural material that is used by humans, such as water, petroleum, minerals, forests, and animals (103)

nonrenewable resource a resource that forms at a rate that is much slower than the rate at which it is consumed (80, 103)

nuclear energy the energy released by a fission or fusion reaction; the binding energy of the atomic nucleus (114)

O

omnivore an organism that eats both plants and animals (9)

open-water zone the zone of a pond or lake that extends from the littoral zone and that is only as deep as light can reach (65)

overpopulation the presence of too many individuals in an area for the available resources (81)

P

parasite an organism that feeds on an organism of another species (the host) and that usually harms the host; the host never benefits from the presence of the parasite

parasitism (PAR uh SIET IZ uhm) a relationship between two species in which one species, the parasite, benefits from the other species, the host, which is harmed (19)

petroleum a liquid mixture of complex hydrocarbon compounds; used widely as a fuel source (107)

pioneer species a species that colonizes an uninhabited area and that starts a process of succession (37)

plankton the mass of mostly microscopic organisms that float or drift freely in freshwater and marine environments (58)

pollution an unwanted change in the environment that is caused by harmful substances, wastes, gases, noise, or radiation (78)

population a group of organisms of the same species that live in a specific geographical area (6)

precipitation any form of water that falls to the Earth's surface from the clouds (32)

predator an organism that eats all or part of another organism (16)

prey an organism that is killed and eaten by another organism (16)

producer an organism that can make its own food by using energy from its surroundings

R

recycling the process of recovering valuable or useful materials from waste or scrap; the process of reusing some items (87, 105)

renewable resource a natural resource that can be replaced at the same rate at which the resource is consumed (80, 103)

S

savanna a grassland that often has scattered trees and that is found in tropical and subtropical areas where seasonal rains, fires, and drought happen (54)

smog photochemical haze that forms when sunlight acts on industrial pollutants and burning fuels (112)

solar energy the energy received by the Earth from the sun in the form of radiation (116)

succession the replacement of one type of community by another at a single location over a period of time (36)

swamp a wetland ecosystem in which shrubs and trees grow (66)

symbiosis a relationship in which two different organisms live in close association with each other (18)

T

tundra a treeless plain found in the Arctic, in the Antarctic, or on the tops of mountains that is characterized by very low winter temperatures and short, cool summers (56)

W

wetland an area of land that is periodically underwater or whose soil contains a great deal of moisture (66)

wind power the use of a windmill to drive an electric generator (117)

Glossary

Spanish Glossary

A

abiotic/abiótico término que describe la parte sin vida del ambiente, incluyendo el agua, las rocas, la luz y la temperatura (4)

acid precipitation/precipitación ácida lluvia, agua-nieve o nieve que contiene una alta concentración de ácidos (112)

B

biodiversity/biodiversidad el número y la variedad de organismos que se encuentran en un área determinada durante un período específico de tiempo (82)

biomass/biomasa materia orgánica que puede ser una fuente de energía; la masa total de los organismos en un área determinada (119)

biome/bioma una región extensa caracterizada por un tipo de clima específico y ciertos tipos de comunidades de plantas y animales (50)

biosphere/biosfera la parte de la Tierra donde existe la vida (7)

biotic/biótico término que describe los factores vivientes del ambiente (4)

C

carnivore/carnívoro un organismo que se alimenta de animales (9)

carrying capacity/capacidad de carga la población más grande que un ambiente puede sostener en cualquier momento dado (15)

chemical energy/energía química la energía que se libera cuando un compuesto químico reacciona para producir nuevos compuestos (116)

coal/carbón un combustible fósil que se forma en el subsuelo a partir de materiales vegetales parcialmente descompuestos (108)

coevolution/coevolución la evolución de dos especies que se debe a su influencia mutua, a menudo de un modo que hace que la relación sea más beneficiosa para ambas (19)

combustion/combustión fenómeno que ocurre cuando una substancia se quema (34)

commensalism/comensalismo una relación entre dos organismos en la que uno se beneficia y el otro no es afectado (18)

community/comunidad todas las poblaciones de especies que viven en el mismo hábitat e interactúan entre sí (6)

condensation/condensación el cambio de estado de gas a líquido (32)

conservation/conservación la preservación y el uso inteligente de los recursos naturales (84)

consumer/consumidor un organismo que se alimenta de otros organismos o de materia orgánica

D

decomposer/descomponedor un organismo que, para obtener energía, desintegra los restos de organismos muertos o los desechos de animales y consume o absorbe los nutrientes

decomposition/descomposición la desintegración de substancias en substancias moleculares más simples (34)

deep-water zone/zona de aguas profundas la zona de un lago o laguna debajo de la zona de aguas abiertas, a donde no llega la luz (65)

desert/desierto una región con poca vegetación o sin vegetación, largos períodos sin lluvia y temperaturas extremas; generalmente se ubica en climas calientes (55)

E

ecology/ecología el estudio de las interacciones de los seres vivos entre sí mismos y entre sí mismos y su ambiente (4)

ecosystem/ecosistema una comunidad de organismos y su ambiente abiótico o no vivo (7)

energy pyramid/pirámide de energía un diagrama triangular que muestra la pérdida de energía en un ecosistema, producida a medida que la energía pasa a través de la cadena alimenticia del ecosistema (11)

estuary/estuario un área donde el agua dulce de los ríos se mezcla con el agua salada del océano (62)

evaporation/evaporación el cambio de una substancia de líquido a gas (32)

F

food chain/cadena alimenticia la vía de transferencia de energía través de varias etapas, que ocurre como resultado de los patrones de alimentación de una serie de organismos (10)

food web/red alimenticia un diagrama que muestra las relaciones de alimentación entre los organismos de un ecosistema (10)

fossil fuel/combustible fósil un recurso energético no renovable formado a partir de los restos de organismos que vivieron hace mucho tiempo (106)

G

gasohol/gasohol una mezcla de gasolina y alcohol que se usa como combustible (119)

geothermal energy/energía geotérmica la energía producida por el calor del interior de la Tierra (120)

H

herbivore/herbívoro un organismo que sólo come plantas (9)

host/huésped el organismo del cual un parásito obtiene alimento y refugio

hydroelectric energy/energía hidroeléctrica energía eléctrica producida por agua en caída (118)

L

littoral zone/zona litoral la zona poco profunda de un lago o una laguna donde la luz llega al fondo y nutre a las plantas (65)

M

marsh/pantano un ecosistema pantanoso sin árboles, donde crecen plantas tales como el pasto (66)

mutualism/mutualismo una relación entre dos especies en la que ambas se benefician (18)

N

natural gas/gas natural una mezcla de hidrocarburos gaseosos que se encuentran debajo de la superficie de la Tierra, normalmente cerca de los depósitos de petróleo, y los cuales se usan como combustible (107)

natural resource/recurso natural cualquier material natural que es utilizado por los seres humanos, como agua, petróleo, minerales, bosques y animales (103)

nonrenewable resource/recurso no renovable un recurso que se forma a una tasa que es mucho más lenta que la tasa a la que se consume (80, 103)

nuclear energy/energía nuclear la energía liberada por una reacción de fisión o fusión; la energía de enlace del núcleo atómico (114)

O

omnivore/omnívoro un organismo que come tanto plantas como animales (9)

open-water zone/zona de aguas superiores la zona de un lago o una laguna que se extiende desde la zona litoral y cuya profundidad sólo alcanza hasta donde penetra la luz (65)

overpopulation/sobrepoblación la presencia de demasiados individuos en un área para los recursos disponibles (81)

P

parasite/parásito un organismo que se alimenta de un organismo de otra especie (el huésped) y que normalmente lo daña; el huésped nunca se beneficia de la presencia del parásito

parasitism/parasitismo una relación entre dos especies en la que una, el parásito, se beneficia de la otra, el huésped, que resulta perjudicada (19)

petroleum/petróleo una mezcla líquida de compuestos hidrocarburos complejos; se usa ampliamente como una fuente de combustible (107)

pioneer species/especie pionera una especie que coloniza un área deshabitada y empieza un proceso de sucesión (37)

plankton/plancton la masa de organismos en su mayoría microscópicos que flotan o se encuentran a la deriva en ambientes de agua dulce o marina (58)

pollution/contaminación un cambio indeseable en el ambiente producido por substancias dañinas, desechos, gases, ruidos o radiación (78)

population/población un grupo de organismos de la misma especie que viven en un área geográfica específica (6)

precipitation/precipitación cualquier forma de agua que cae de las nubes a la superficie de la Tierra (32)

predator/depredador un organismo que se alimenta de otro organismo o de parte de él (16)

prey/presa un organismo al que otro organismo mata para alimentarse de él (16)

producer/productor un organismo que puede elaborar sus propios alimentos utilizando la energía de su entorno

R

recycling/reciclar el proceso de recuperar materiales valiosos o útiles de los desechos o de la basura; el proceso de reutilizar algunas cosas (87, 105)

renewable resource/recurso renovable un recurso natural que puede reemplazarse a la misma tasa a la que se consume (80, 103)

S

savanna/sabana una región de pastizales que, a menudo, tiene árboles dispersos; se encuentra en áreas tropicales y subtropicales donde se producen lluvias, incendios y sequías estacionales (54)

smog/esmog bruma fotoquímica que se forma cuando la luz solar actúa sobre contaminantes industriales y combustibles (112)

solar energy/energía solar la energía que la Tierra recibe del Sol en forma de radiación (116)

succession/sucesión el reemplazo de un tipo de comunidad por otro en un mismo lugar a lo largo de un período de tiempo (36)

swamp/ciénaga un ecosistema de pantano en el que crecen arbustos y árboles (66)

symbiosis/simbiosis una relación en la que dos organismos diferentes viven estrechamente asociados uno con el otro (18)

T

tundra/tundra una llanura sin árboles situada en la región ártica o antártica o en la cumbre de las montañas; se caracteriza por temperaturas muy bajas en el invierno y veranos cortos y frescos (56)

W

wetland/pantano un área de tierra que está periódicamente bajo el agua o cuyo suelo contiene una gran cantidad de humedad (66)

wind power/potencia eólica el uso de un molino de viento para hacer funcionar un generador eléctrico (117)

Index

Boldface page numbers refer to illustrative material, such as figures, tables, margin elements, photographs, and illustrations.

A

abiotic factors, 4, **4**, 50
acacia trees, ants and, 19, **19**
acid precipitation, 112, **112**
adding fractions, 150
air pollution, 112, **112**
alcohol, as fuel, 119, **119**
algae
    blooms, 42
    mutualism with corals, 18, **18**
    as producers, 8
    in the Sargasso Sea, 63
Alonso-Mejía, Alfonso, 75
alpine tundra, 56, **56**
alternative energy resources, 114–121
    biomass, 119, **119**
    fission, 114–115, **114, 115**
    fuel cells, 116, **116**
    fusion, 115, **115**, 129
    gasohol, 119, **119**
    geothermal, 120, **120**
    hydroelectric, 118, **118**, 128
    hydrogen fuels, 98
    solar, 116–117, **116, 117**
    wind, 117, **117**
amino acids
ammonia, 40–41
animals
    as consumers, **8–9,** 9, 10, **10**
    diversity of, 82
anthracite, 110, **110**
ants, 19, **19**
area, **151**
Australia, coevolution in, **20**
averages, 148

B

bacteria (singular, *bacterium*)
    as decomposers, 9, **9**
    intestinal, 28
    nitrogen fixation by, 34, **34**
    as producers, **8**
bananas, 88, **88**
barium, **114**
bats, pollination by, 20, **20**

Begay, Fred, 129, **129**
benthic zone, 61, **61**
biodegradable plastics, 85, **85**
biodiversity, 82, **82**
    habitat destruction and, 82, **82,** 89
    lab on, 92–93
    maintaining, 88–89, **88, 89**
    in mature communities, 39, **39**
biomass, 119, **119**
biomes, 50, **50**
    alpine tundra, 56, **56**
    coniferous forests, 52, **52**
    deserts, 55, **55**
    global distribution of, **50**
    grasslands, 54, **54**
    polar tundra, 56
    savannas, 54, **54**
    temperate deciduous forests, 51, **51**
    tropical rain forests, 53, **53**, 82
biosphere, 5, **5**, 7, **7**
biotic factors, 4, **4,** 50
bison, **54**
bituminous coal, 110, **110**
Blackfooted penguins, 112, **112**
black gold, 107
booklet instructions (FoldNote), 141, **141**
British Thermal Units (BTU), 114
butane, 107
butterflies, 75

C

cactuses, **55**
calcium, 35
California condor, 88, **88**
camouflage, 17
canopies, 53, **53**
carbon, in coal, 110, **110**
carbon cycle, 33–34, **33**
carbon dioxide, **35**, 79
carnivores, **8**, 9, 9
carrying capacity, 15, **15,** 22
cars, **116,** 128
CFCs, 79, **79**
chain-of-events chart instructions (Graphic Organizer), 145, **145**
chemical energy, 116, **116**
chemical wastes, 79
Chernobyl nuclear release, 115

climate, mountains and, **54**
climate change, **35,** 79
climax species, 39, **39**
coal, 108, **108**
    acid precipitation from, 112
    coal-burning power plants, 108
    formation of, 110, **110**
    location of, 111, **111**
    mining of, 112
    types of, 110, **110**
coal-burning power plants, 108, **108**
coevolution, 19, **19, 20**
combustion, **33**, 34, **34**
commensalism, 18, **18**
communities, 5, **5**, 6, **6**. *See also* ecosystems; interactions of living things
comparison table instructions (Graphic Organizer), 144, **144**
competition, 15
composting, 85
concept map instructions (Graphic Organizer), 145, **145**
conclusions, drawing, 147
condensation, 32, **32**
condors, 88, **88**
coniferous forests, 52, **52**
conservation of resources, 84, **84,** 104–105, **105**
consumers, **8–9,** 9–10, **10**
control groups, 147
controlled experiments, 147
coral reefs, 62, **62**
corals, 18, **18**, 62
corn, gasohol from, 119, **119**
cross-multiplication, 148
crude oil, 107
cubes, surface area and volume of, 153
cycles in nature, 30–31
    calcium and phosphorus, 35
    carbon, 33–34, **33**
    ecological succession, 36–39, **36, 37, 38, 39**
    nitrogen, 34–35, **34,** 40–41
    water, 32–33, **32**

D

deciduous forests, 51, **51**
decimals, 151
decomposers, 9, **9**
decomposition, **33,** 34, **34**, 35, 40–41
deep sea volcanic vents, 61, **61,** 74

Index

deep-water zone, 65, **65**
deep zone, oceanic, **59**
defensive chemicals, 17
deforestation, 82
desalination, 42
deserts, 55, **55**
deuterium, **115**
diversity, of animals, 82, 89. *See
    also* biodiversity
dividing fractions, 150
Dockery, Dalton, 29
dogs, 28
double door instructions
    (FoldNote), 140, **140**
drinking water, 80, **80,** 90
dung, as fuel, 119, **119**

E

ecological succession, 36–39, **36,
    37, 38, 39**
ecologists, 75
ecology, 2–21, **4, 5, 6**
ecosystems, 5, **5,** 7, **7,** 50–67. *See
    also* interactions of living
    things
    biodiversity in, 39, **39,** 92–93
    biome distribution, **50**
    desert biomes, 55, **55**
    energy movement through,
        10–11, **10, 11**
    forest biomes, 51–53, **51, 52, 53**
    freshwater, 64–67, **64, 65, 66**
    grassland biomes, 54, **54**
    marine, 58–63, **58, 59, 60–61,
        62**
    mark-recapture counting
        method, 10–11, **10, 11**
    stream and river, 64, **64**
    transition from lake to forest, 67
    tundra biomes, 56, **56**
    wolves in, 12–13, **12**
electrical energy
    from fossil fuels, 106, **106,** 108,
        108
    from geothermal energy, 120,
        120
    in satellite photo of U.S., **106**
endangered species, 88, **88,** 98
Endangered Species Act, 88–89
energy, 102–121
    alternative sources of, 85, **85,**
        89, 98
    chemical, 116, **116**
    electrical, 106, **106,** 108, **108,**
        120
    from fission, 114–115, **114, 115**
    from fusion, 115, **115,** 129
    geothermal, 120, **120**
    hydroelectric, 118, **118,** 128

movement through ecosystems,
    10–11, **10, 11**
solar, 116–117, **116, 117**
units of, 114
from waste-to-energy plants, 87,
    87
energy connections
    consumers, **8–9,** 9–10, **10**
    decomposers, 9, **9**
    energy pyramids, 11–13, **11**
    food chains and webs, 4–7, 10,
        10
    producers, 8, **8–9**
energy pyramids, 11–13, **11, 13**
energy resources
    biomass, 119, **119**
    coal, 108, **108**
    conserving, 104–105, **105**
    fission, 114–115, **114, 115**
    fuel cells, 116, **116**
    fusion, 115, **115,** 129
    gasohol, 119, **119**
    geothermal, 120, **120**
    hydroelectric, 118, **118,** 128
    labs on, **109,** 122–123
    natural gas, 107, **107**
    petroleum, 107, **107**
    pollution from, 112, **112**
    renewable *vs.* nonrenewable,
        103, **103**
    solar, 116–117, **116, 117**
    wind power, 117, **117**
environmental problems, 78–83
    carbon dioxide, **35,** 79
    chemicals, 79
    effects on humans, 83
    garbage, 78, **78**
    habitat destruction, 82, **82**
    human population growth, 81,
        81
    introduced species, 81, **81**
    noise, 80
    radioactive wastes, 79
    resource depletion, 80, **80**
Environmental Protection Agency
    (EPA), 89
environmental solutions, 84–91
    conservation, 84, **84**
    maintaining biodiversity,
        88–89, **88, 89**
    recycling, 87, **87**
    reducing waste and pollution,
        85, **85**
    reusing materials, 86, **86**
    strategies, 89
    what you can do, 90, **90**
EPA (Environmental Protection
    Agency), 89

estuaries, 62, **62**
evaporation, 32, **32**
evergreen forests, 52, **52**
exotic species, 81, **81**
experimental groups, 147
Exxon Valdez oil spill, **82,** 99

F

Fan, Michael, 43
ferns, in ecological succession, **37**
fertilizers, 68–69, 79, **79**
fishes, 16
fission, 114–115, **114, 115**
flowers, 20, **20**
FoldNote instructions, 140–143,
    140, 141, 142, 143
follicle mites, 28
food
    energy pyramids, 11–13, **11**
    food chains and webs, 4–7, 10,
        10, 13
food chains, 10, **10**
food pyramids (energy pyramids),
    11–13, **11**
food webs, 10, **10,** 13
forest biomes, 51–53, **51, 52, 53**
forest fires, 36, **36**
forests
    canopies, 53, **53**
    coniferous, 52, **52**
    deciduous, 51, **51**
    deforestation, 82
    rain forests, 53, **53,** 82
    regrowth of, 36, **36**
fossil fuels, 106–113, **106**
    coal, 108, **108**
    formation of, 109–110, **109, 110**
    lab on, **109**
    location of, 111, **111**
    natural gas, 107, **107,** 109, **109,**
        111
    obtaining, 111, **111**
    petroleum, 107, **107,** 109, **109,**
        111–112
    problems with, 112, **112**
four-corner fold instructions
    (FoldNote), 142, **142**
fractionation, **107**
fractions, 149–150
freshwater ecosystems, 64–67
    lab on, **65**
    pond and lake, 65, **65**
    stream and river, 64, **64**
    transition from lake to forest, 67
    wetland, 66, **66**
fuel cells, 116, **116**
fungi (singular, *fungus*), **9,** 37
fusion, 115, **115,** 129

Index

G

garbage, 78, **78,** 87
gasohol, 119, **119**
GCF (greatest common factor), 149
generation time, 28
geothermal energy, 120, **120**
The Geysers power plant, 120
glaciers, primary succession after, 37, **37**
global warming, **35,** 79
goldenrod spiders, 16, **16**
Graphic Organizer instructions, 144–145, **144, 145**
grassland biomes, 54, **54**
gray wolves, 12–13, **12,** 98
greatest common factor (GCF), 149
groundwater, 32, **32**
Gulf of Mexico, 42

H

habitats, 82, **82,** 89, **89**
hair, 99
hair follicles, 28
hazardous wastes, 78
helium, **115**
herbivores, **8,** 9, **9**
holdfasts, 62
horticultural specialists, 29
hosts, 19, **19,** 28
human population growth, 81, **81**
hummingbirds, 20
humpback whales, **58**
hybrid cars, 128
hydrocarbons, 107, **108**
hydroelectric energy, 118, **118,** 128
hydrogen-fueled cars, 85, 98
hydrogen isotopes, **115**
hydrothermal vents, 61, **61,** 74
hypotheses, 146–147
hypoxia, 42

I

Industrial Revolution, 78
integumentary system, 99
interactions of living things, 2–3. *See also* ecosystems
    biotic *vs.* abiotic parts of environment, 4, **4,** 14
    coevolution, 19, **19, 20**
    competition, 15
    consumers, **8–9,** 9–10, **10**
    decomposers, 9, **9**
    energy pyramids, 11–13, **11**
    with the environment, 14–15
    food chains and webs, 4–7, 10, **10**
    lab on, **5**
    levels of environmental organiza- tion, 5–7, **5, 6**
    predators and prey, 12, 16–17, **16**
    producers, 8, **8–9**
    symbiosis, 18–19, **18, 19**
intertidal zone, 60, **60**
introduced species, 81, **81**
isotopes of hydrogen, **115**

J

jack rabbits, **55**
joules, 114

K

kangaroo rats, **55**
key-term fold instructions (FoldNote), 142, **142**
krypton, 114

L

lake ecosystems, 65, **65,** 67–69
land biomes, 50–57
layered book instructions (FoldNote), 141, **141**
least common denominator (LCD), 150
lichens, 37
light, ocean depth and, 60–61, **60–61**
lignite, 110, **110**
limiting factors, 14–15
liquefied natural gas, 107, **107**
littoral zone, 65, **65**

M

marine ecosystems, 58–63
    coral reefs, 62, **62**
    depth and sunlight, 60–61, **60–61**
    depth and temperature, 59, **59**
    estuaries, 62, **62**
    intertidal areas, 62, **62**
    plankton, 58, **58**
    polar ice, 63
    pollution and, 82, **82**
    Sargasso Sea, 63
mark-recapture method, 22–23
marshes, 66–67, **66**
Math Refresher, 148–149
matter, 32–35
mature communities, 39, **39**
McCrory, Phil, 99
megawatts (MWe), 114
methane, 107
mimicry, **17**
mining, 111–112
mites, 28
monarch butterflies, 75
mosses, 37
mountains, climate and, **54**
multiplying fractions, 150
mutualism, **18,** 18–19

N

National Aeronautics and Space Administration (NASA), 99
Native Americans, 129
natural gardening, 29
natural gas, 107, **107**
    formation of, 109, **109**
    location of, 111, **111**
natural resources, 102–105
    conservation of, 104–105, **105**
    examples of, **102**
    renewable *vs.* nonrenewable, 80, **80,** 103, **103**
Navajos, 129
neritic zone, 60, **60**
nitrates, 68–69
nitrogen
    fixation, 34, **34**
    nitrates, 68–69
    nitrogen cycle, 34–35, **34,** 40–41
noise pollution, 80
nonpoint-source pollution, 82
nonrenewable resources, 80, **80,** 103, **103**
northern snakehead fish, 81, **81**
notetaking, 144–145
nuclear energy, 114, **114**
    fission, 114–115, **114, 115**
    fusion, 115, **115,** 129
    radioactive wastes from, 115

nuclear fusion, 115, **115,** 129
nuclear wastes, 79, 115
nutrients, water pollution from, 68–69

O

oceanic vents, 61, **61,** 74
oceanic zone, 61, **61**
oceans
    coral reefs, 62, **62**
    depth and sunlight, 60–61, **60–99**
    depth and temperature, 59, **59**
    estuaries, 62
    hydrothermal vents, 61, **61,** 74
    intertidal areas, 62, **62**
    polar ice, 63
    Sargasso Sea, 63
oil spills, 82, **82,** 99, 112, **112**
omnivores, 9
open-water zone, 65, **65**
organic farming, 85
organisms, 5, **5**
overpopulation, 81, **81**
oxygen, lack of, 42
ozone, 79, **79**
ozone holes, **79**

P

painted turtles, **66**
pampas, 54, **54**
parasitism, 19, **19**
PCBs, 79
peat, 110, **110**
penguins, 112, **112**
percentages, 149
permafrost, 56
permeability, 109, **109**
permeable rocks, 109, **109**
pesticides, 89
petroleum, 107, **107**
    crude oil, 107
    formation of, 109, **109**
    location of, 111, **111**
    obtaining, 111, **111**
    oil spills, 112, **112**
phosphates, 68–69
phosphorous cycling, 35
photosynthesis, 8, **8,** 33, **33**
pioneer species, 37, **37**
pitohui, **17**
plankton, 58, **58,** 62
plants, as producers, 8, **8**
plastics, 82, 85, **85**
point-source pollution, 82
polar ice, 63

polar tundra, 56
pollination, coevolution and, 20, **20**
pollution, 78, **78.** See also environmental solutions
    carbon dioxide, **35,** 79
    chemicals, 79
    effects on humans, 83
    from fossil fuels, 112, **112**
    garbage, 78, **78**
    noise, 80
    from oil spills, 112, **112**
    point-source vs. nonpoint-source, 82
    radioactive wastes, 79
    water, 104
pond ecosystems, 65, **65,** 67–69
population growth, 81, **81**
populations, 5–6, **5, 6,** 14. See also interactions of living things
    competition between, 15
    human population growth, 81, **81**
    interactions with environment, 14–15
    lab on, 22–23
    mark-recapture counting method, 22–23
    rabbits in Australia, **20**
power plants
    coal-burning, 108
    fission, 114–115, **114, 115**
    geothermal, 120, **120**
    hydroelectric, 118, **118,** 128
prairie dogs, 11, **11**
prairies, 54, **54**
precipitation, 32, **32**
predators, 12, 16–17, **16**
predictions from hypotheses, 146
prey, 16–17, **16**
primary succession, 37, **37**
prisms, volume formula for, 151
producers, 8, **8–9**
propane, 107, **108**
proportions, 148
pyramid instructions (FoldNote), 140, **140**

R

rabbits, **20**
radioactive wastes, 79, 115
rainfall
    in desert biomes, **55**
    in forest biomes, **51, 52, 53**
    in grassland biomes, **54**
    in tundra biomes, **56**
rain forests, 53, **53,** 82
ratios, 148
reclaimed wastewater, 86, **86**
rectangle, area of, 151
recycling, 87, **87,** 105, **105**

Reduce, Reuse, and Recycle, 84, **84**
reducing fractions, 149
reducing waste and pollution, 84–85, **85.** See also environmental solutions
refineries, 107, **107**
remoras, 18, **18**
renewable resources, 80, **80,** 103, **103**
resource depletion, 80, **80**
resource recovery, 87, **87**
resources, 80, **80**
resources, natural, 102–105, **103**
    conservation of, 104–105, **105**
    examples of, **102**
    renewable vs. nonrenewable, 103
respiration, in carbon cycle, 33, **33**
reusing materials, 86, **86**
rivers, 64, **64**
rock, permeable, 109, **109**
runoff, 32, **32**

S

salt marsh community, **6**
Sargasso Sea, 63
savannas, 54, **54**
Scarlet king snakes, **17**
scavengers, 9, **9**
schools, of fishes, 16
scientific methods, 146–147, **146, 147**
scientific notation, 151
secondary succession, 38, **38**
sedimentation, 67
sharks, 18, **18**
smog, 112, **112**
solar collectors, 117, **117**
solar energy, 85, **85,** 116–117, **116, 117**
solutions, environmental, 84–91
    conservation, 84, **84**
    maintaining biodiversity, 88–89, **88, 89**
    recycling, 87, **87**
    reducing waste and pollution, 85, **85**
    reusing materials, 86, **86**
    strategies, 89
    what you can do, 90, **90**
Sonoran Desert, **39**
spider map instructions (Graphic Organizer), 144, **144**
square, area of, 151
steppes, 54, **54**
streams, 64, **64**
strip mining, 80, **80,** 111
subtracting fractions, 150
succession, ecological, 36–39, **36, 37, 38, 39**

Index

surface coal mining, 111
surface zone, oceanic, **59**
swamps, 66–67, **66**
symbiosis, 18–19, **18, 19**

T

table fold instructions (FoldNote),
143, **143**
temperate deciduous forests, 51, **51**
temperate grasslands, 54, **54**
temperature
  in deserts, **55**
  in forest biomes, **51, 52, 53**
  global warming and, **35,** 79
  in grassland biomes, 54
  ocean depth and, 59, **59**
  in thermal vents, 74
  in tundra, **56**
thermal vents, 61, **61,** 74
thermocline, **59**
Three Gorges dam (China), 129
three-panel flip chart instructions
  (FoldNote), 142, **142**
tomato hornworms, 19, **19**
transpiration, **32,** 33
trash, 78, **78**, 87, **87**
Treasure oil spill, 112, **112**
tree line, 56
triangle, area of, 151
tributaries, **64**
tri-fold instructions (FoldNote), 143,
  143
tritium, **115**
tropical rain forests, 53, **53,** 82
tundra biomes, 56, **56**
turbines, wind, **102,** 117, **117**
two-panel flip chart instructions
  (FoldNote), 143, **143**

U

ultraviolet (UV) radiation, ozone
  and, **79**
units of energy, 114
uranium, 114–115, **114**

V

viruses, coevolution of, **20**
volume, 151

W

warning coloration, 16–17, **16, 17**
wastes
  chemical, 79
  hazardous, 78
  radioactive, 79
  reclaimed wastewater, 86, **86**
  reducing, 85, **85**
  trash, 78, **78**, 87, **87**
  waste-to-energy plants, 87, **87**
  wastewater treatment, 43
waste-to-energy plants, 87, **87**
wastewater reclamation, 86, **86**
wastewater treatment, 43

water
  desalination, 42
  fresh water, **33,** 42, **80**
  freshwater ecosystems, 64–67,
    64, 65, 66
  groundwater, 32, **32**
  hydroelectric energy from, 118,
    118, 128
  importance to humans, 90
  pollution, 104
  resource depletion, 80, **80,** 86
  water cycle, 32–33, **32**
water cycle, 32–33, **32**
water wheels, 118, **118,** 122–123
web of life, 4–7, 10, **10**. *See also*
  interactions of living things
weeds, in secondary succession, **38**
wetlands, 66–67, **66,** 74
whales, humpback, **58**
wind power, 117, **117**
wind turbines, **102,** 117, **117**
wolves, 12–13, **12,** 98

Y

yellow jackets, **17**
Yellowstone National Park
  ecological succession at, 36, **36**
  elk population in, **15**
  gray wolf reintroduction, 12–13

Index

Credits

Abbreviations used: (t) top, (c) center, (b) bottom, (l) left, (r) right, (bkgd) background

PHOTOGRAPHY

Front Cover Faulkner/Corbis

Skills Practice Lab Teens Sam Dudgeon/HRW

Connection to Astronomy Corbis Images; **Connection to Biology** David M. Phillips/Visuals Unlimited; **Connection to Chemistry** Digital Image copyright © 2005 PhotoDisc; **Connection to Environment** Digital Image copyright © 2005 PhotoDisc; **Connection to Geology** Letraset Phototone; **Connection to Language Arts** Digital Image copyright © 2005 PhotoDisc; **Connection to Meteorology** Digital Image copyright © 2005 PhotoDisc; **Connection to Oceanography** © ICONOTEC; **Connection to Physics** Digital Image copyright © 2005 PhotoDisc

Table of Contents v (tr), © Jeff Hunter/Getty Images/The Image Bank; v (bl), James Randklev/Getty Images/Stone; vi–vii, Victoria Smith/HRW; x (bl), Sam Dudgeon/HRW; xi (tl), John Langford/HRW; xi (b), Sam Dudgeon/HRW; xii (tl), Victoria Smith/HRW; xii (bl), Stephanie Morris/HRW; xii (br), Sam Dudgeon/HRW; xiii (tl), Patti Murray/Animals, Animals; xiii (tr), Jana Birchum/HRW; xiii (b), Peter Van Steen/HRW

Chapter One 2–3 © Roine Magnusson/Getty Images/The Image Bank; 9 (r), © David M. Phillips/Visuals Unlimited; 11 (t), © George H. H. Huey/CORBIS; 11 (c), © D. Robert & Lorri Franz/CORBIS; 11 (b), © Jason Brindel Photography/Alamy Photos; 12 (t), © Naturfoto Honal/CORBIS; 12 (b), Jeff Lepore/Photo Researchers; 14 Jeff Foott/AUSCAPE; 15 © Ross Hamilton/Getty Images/Stone; 16 (l), Visuals Unlimited/Gerald & Buff Corsi; 16 (cr), Hans Pfletschinger/Peter Arnold; 17 (r), W. Peckover/Academy of Natural Sciences Philadelphia/VIREO; 17 (l), Leroy Simon/Visuals Unlimited; 18 (b), Ed Robinson/Tom Stack & Associates; 18 (tl), © Telegraph Color Library/Getty Images/FPG International; 18 (tr), OSF/Peter Parks/Animals Animals Earth Scenes; 19 (t), © Gay Bumgarner/Getty Images/Stone; 19 (b), Carol Hughes/Bruce Coleman; 20 (tl), CSIRO Wildlife & Ecology; 20 (r), © Rick & Nora Bowers/Visuals Unlimited; 21 Leroy Simon/Visuals Unlimited; 22 Sam Dudgeon/HRW; 23 Sam Dudgeon/HRW; 23 Sam Dudgeon/HRW; 24 Leroy Simon/Visuals Unlimited; 28 (r), © National Geographic Image Collection/Darlyne Murawski; 28 (l), Digital Image copyright © 2005 PhotoDisc; 29 (r), Photo from the Dept. of Communication Services, North Carolina State University; 29 (l), Digital Image copyright © 2005 Artville

Chapter Two 30–31 © Bryan and Cherry Alexander Photography; 36 (l), Diana L. Stratton/Tom Stack & Associates; 36 (r), © Stan Osolinski; 39 Kim Heacox/DRK Photo; 40 Sam Dudgeon/HRW; 41 (br), Sam Dudgeon/HRW; 41 (bl), Sam Dudgeon/HRW; 41 (t), Sam Dudgeon/HRW; 46 (t), Reed Saxon/AP/Wide World Photos; 47 (t), Neil Michel/Axiom; 47 (b), Neil Michel/Axiom

Chapter Three 48–49 © Studio Carlo Dani/Animals Animals/Earth Scenes; 54 (t), Grant Heilman; 54 (b), Tom Brakefield/Bruce Coleman; 56 (t), © Kathy Bushue/Getty Images/Stone; 58–59 (b), Stuart Westmorland/Getty Images/Stone; 58 (inset), Manfred Kage/Peter Arnold; 62 (b), © Jeff Hunter/Getty Images/The Image Bank; 66 (t), Dwight Kuhn; 66 (b), Hardie Truesdale/International Stock; 69 Sam Dudgeon/HRW; 74 (r), Dr. Verena Tunnicliffe; 74 (l), © Raymond Gehman/CORBIS; 75 (t), Lincoln P. Brower; 75 (b), © Royalty–Free/CORBIS

Chapter Four 76–77 Martin Harvey/NHPA; 78 Larry Lefever/Grant Heilman Photography; 79 (t), J. Roche/Peter Arnold, Inc.; 79 (b), NASA; 80 (b), © Jacques Jangoux/Getty Images/Stone; 81 REUTERS/Jonathan Searle/NewsCom; 82 © Rex Ziak/Getty Images/Stone; 83 REUTERS/Jonathan Searle/NewsCom; 84 (l), Peter Van Steen/HRW; 84 (c), Peter Van Steen/HRW; 84 (r), Peter Van Steen/HRW; 85 (t), Argonne National Laboratory; 85 (b), Digital Image copyright © 2005 PhotoDisc; 86 (b), PhotoEdit; 86 (l), Kay Park–Rec Corp.; 87 (t), Peter Van Steen/HRW; 87 (b), Martin Bond/Science Photo Library/Photo Researchers; 88 (b), K. W. Fink/Bruce Coleman; 88 (t), © Sindre Ellingsen/Alamy Photos; 89 Stephen J. Krasemann/DRK Photo; 90 (bl), Sam Dudgeon/HRW; 90 (t), © Will & Deni McIntyre/Getty Images/Stone; 90 (br), Stephen J. Krasemann/DRK Photo; 91 (t), K. W. Fink/Bruce Coleman; 92 Peter Van Steen/HRW; 93 (tl), Tom Bean/DRK Photo; 93 (tr), Darrell Gulin/DRK Photo; 94 (l), Peter Van Steen/HRW; 94 (r), Peter Van Steen/HRW; 95 Larry Lefever/Grant Heilman Photography; 98 (l), Art Wolfe; 98 (r), © Toru Yamanaka/AFP/CORBIS; 99 (b), John S. Lough/Visuals Unlimited; 99 (t), Huntsville Times

Chapter Five 100 (inset), Roger Ressmeyer/CORBIS; 100–101 (inset), Novovitch/Liaison/Getty Images; 102 (tc), Andy Christiansen/HRW; 102 (tl), © Russell Illiq/Photodisc/Getty Images; 102 (tr), Mark Lewis/Getty Images/Stone; 103 (tl), James Randklev/Getty Images/Stone; 103 (b), Ed Malles/Liaison/Newsmakers/Getty Images; 103 (tr), Myrleen Furgusson Cate/PhotoEdit; 104, Victoria Smith/HRW; 106, Data courtesy Marc Imhoff of NASA/GSFC and Christopher Elvidge of NOAA/NGDC. Image by Craig Mayhew and Robert Simmon, NASA/GSFC.; 107 (b), John Zoiner; 107 (t), Mark Green/Getty Images/Taxi; 108, John Zoiner; 110, 2, Paolo Koch/Photo Researchers, Inc.; 110, 1, Horst Schafer/Peter Arnold, Inc.; 110, 3, Brian Parker/Tom Stack & Associates; 110, 4, C. Kuhn/Getty Images/The Image Bank; 111 (br), Alberto Incrocci/Getty Images/The Image Bank; 112 (inset), ©1994 NYC Parks Photo Archive/Fundamental Photographs; 112 (tl), © 1994 Kristen Brochmann/Fundamental Photographs; 112, Martin Harvey; 115 (tr), Tom Myers/Photo Researchers, Inc; 116 (t), Laurent Gillieron/Keystone/AP/Wide World Photos; 117 (b), Terry W. Eggers/CORBIS; 118 (t), Craig Sands/National Geographic Image Collection/Getty Images; 118 (b), Caio Coronel/Reuters/NewsCom; 119, G.R. Roberts Photo Library; 121, Laurent Gillieron/Keystone/AP/Wide World Photos; 123, Sam Dudgeon/HRW; 124, HRW; 125; 112, Martin Harvey; 128 (t), Junko Kimura/Getty Images; 128 (b), STR/AP/Wide World Photos; 129 (t), Courtesy of Los Alamos National Laboratories; 129 (b), Corbis Images

Lab Book/Appendix "LabBook Header", "L", Corbis Images; "a", Letraset Phototone; "b", and "B", HRW; "o", and "k", images ©2006 PhotoDisc/HRW; 132 Peter Van Steen/HRW; 133 (tr), © Digital Vision/Getty Images; 133 (cl), Visuals Unlimited/Doug Sokell; 133 (br), Larry Nielsen/Peter Arnold; 133 (bl), Phil Degginger; 135 Peter Van Steen/HRW; 137 Sam Dudgeon/HRW; 141 Sam Dudgeon/HRW; 142 Sam Dudgeon/HRW; 147 (t), Peter Van Steen/HRW; 147 (b), Sam Dudgeon/HRW